Idealism and Liberal Education

Idealism
and
Liberal Education

James O. Freedman

Ann Arbor
THE UNIVERSITY OF MICHIGAN PRESS

Copyright © by the University of Michigan 1996
All rights reserved
Published in the United States of America by
The University of Michigan Press
Manufactured in the United States of America

1999   1998   1997   1996   4   3   2   1

A CIP catalog record for this book is available from the British Library.

Library of Congress Cataloging-in-Publication Data

Freedman, James O.
    Idealism and liberal education / James O. Freedman.
      p. cm.
    ISBN 0-472-10692-9 (alk. paper)
    1. Education, Humanistic—United States.   2. Idealism.
    3. Education, Higher—United States—Aims and objectives.
    I. Title.
    LC1011.F72   1996
    370.11′2′0973—dc20   95-41674
                                          CIP

For my family
Sheba, Deborah, and Jared

Contents

Introduction   1

1. **Life and Letters**

Becoming an Educator   9
The Joys of Collecting Books   31
A Dukedom Large Enough   43
Presidential Prose   49
The Stillness and the Courage   51

2. **Content and Character in Liberal Education**

The Teaching of Values in a Liberal Education   55
The Promise of Equality   61
The Organization of Knowledge   69
Science and Liberal Learning   77
Liberal Education and the Legal Profession   81
The Lessons of the Law   93
The Professor's Life   99

3. **Models for Shaping a Life**

Public Selves, Private Selves   105
The Power of Idealism   111
The Value of Intellectuals   115
Insiders and Outsiders   119
Thurgood Marshall: Man of Character   129
The Capacity of Imagination   145
Originals and Copies   149
Those Who Are Truly Great   155
Ordinary Backgrounds, Extraordinary Men   161
Essayists and Solitude   167

Index   173

Introduction

This is a book about liberal education and its goals. It reflects my experience as president of the University of Iowa, from 1982 to 1987, and as president of Dartmouth College, since 1987. It rests on my belief that liberal education is the surest instrument yet devised for developing those civilizing qualities of mind and character that enable men and women to lead satisfying lives and to make significant contributions to society.

Several years ago John Kenneth Galbraith said that universities are becoming, at the end of the century, what banks were at the beginning: the suppliers of the nation's most needed source of capital. Society's need for liberally educated men and women has never been greater than it is today, as we ponder still the transforming horror of the Holocaust, as we live daily with the awesome potential of modern science, as we strive to avoid the perils of the post–cold war world, as we experience the awful anguish of failing to meet the simple imperative of feeding all the peoples of our planet.

Why is liberal education so important? A liberal education acquaints students with the cultural achievements of the past and prepares them for the exigencies of an unforeseeable future. It provides them with standards by which to measure human achievement. It fires their minds with new ideas—powerful and transcendent ideas that will trouble them, elevate them, and brace them for new endeavors. It offers students an opportunity to develop the humane empathy and moral courage required to endure uncertainty, disappointment, and suffering.

A liberal education also stirs students to probe the mysteries of the natural world, to reflect on the rise and fall of cultures, to find meaning in the enduring achievements of Western and Eastern civilizations, and to consider the ambiguities and arguable lessons of human history. And it awakens them to the power of art to shape, question, and impose order on human experience and human destiny, to express the hopes and despairs, the dreams and nightmares of the human condition.

Further, a liberal education encourages students to seek the affirmation of their most authentic selves. It sets in motion a process of critical examination and imaginative introspection that leads students toward personal definition. It helps students to develop an independent perspective for reflecting on the nature and the texture of their lives. And it inspires students to delineate the foundations of their moral identity and to find their distinctive ways through the complicated and uncertain process by which intellectual and moral maturation occurs.

More than any historical datum, any experimental result, or any textual explication, a liberal education conveys to students a sense of joy in learning—joy in participating in the life of the mind; joy in achieving competence and mastery; joy in entering the adult world of obligations, intimacies, and relationships; joy in engaging in the converse among our several generations.

Finally, a liberal education invites students to explore the ordeal of being human—the drama of discovering the darker side of the self; the responsibility of imposing meaning on one's life and one's society; the challenge of transcending the ambiguity-entangled counsel of arrogance and modesty, egotism and altruism, emotion and reason, opportunism and loyalty, individualism and conformity.

At the heart of a liberal education lies a conception of intellectual wholeness, an ideal of coherence within that expanding array of specialties and subspecialties, of disciplines and subdisciplines, that composes the universe of knowledge. But that conception of wholeness has been threatened by this century's widening separations between literature and politics, science and religion, reason and faith, tradition and experimentation.

Too often, the increasing tendency toward specialization has had fragmenting consequences for the life of the mind. It has sheltered men and women of broad-ranging imagination behind narrowly drawn disciplinary bounds, thereby discouraging them from becoming educated in the fullest sense of that term. It has reduced the opportunities for collegial discourse among different departments and disciplines, as the faculty and students have become the masters of material of more slender scope. And it has denied faculty and students an understanding of the premises and assumptions of disciplines other than their own, thereby inhibiting inquiry across disciplinary lines. We need to regain that sense of intellectual wholeness that characterizes liberal education at its finest.

In a parallel development, students today face substantial pressures toward vocationalism at too preliminary a stage in their developing lives. They are told on virtually every side that they must make an early commitment to a specific career. These pressures threaten to diminish the value of their college years and defeat the function of a liberal education. It is the responsibility of institutions of liberal learning to fortify students to resist these social pressures toward premature vocationalism, to serve as champions of the primacy of the liberal arts and the life of the mind.

In surveying the purposes of liberal education, one cannot ignore the essential role that colleges play in preparing students for the responsibilities of citizenship and leadership. Liberal education has an historic obligation to train the leaders of this nation, persons whose wisdom, skill, and character will build the sense of community on which the maintenance of our democratic institutions and the fabric of our social life depend.

I have great faith in today's undergraduates. I do not share the conventional wisdom that today's generation of college students lacks idealism and seeks only prevocational education, in the heady pursuit of material success. Perhaps such pessimism has always been present. (Henry Adams, in reflecting on his own college commencement in 1858, observed, "If any one of us has had an ambition higher than that of making money; a motive better than that of expediency; a faith warmer than that of reasoning; a love purer than that of self; he has been slow to express it; still slower to urge it.") Yet I believe that today's undergraduates possess an untapped capacity for idealism and altruism, for which our society does not provide adequate outlets. They are not so much indifferent to idealism as uninspired by their elders, not so much misled in their values as left to flounder on their own.

Part of the task of training the leaders of tomorrow is to nurture in students a sense of idealism, a sense of personal destiny, a sense that service counts in meeting the daunting tasks that confront us. Reverend Martin Luther King, Jr., once said, "Everybody can be great because everybody can serve."

As the president first of a large public university and now of a small private college, I have made it my practice to speak to students about the importance of idealists—men and women who, by the way they have lived their lives and by the impressive weight of their achievements, have been formative influences on my own personal and intellectual development. I have spoken about some of my heroes and heroines: Flannery O'Connor and Eudora Welty, Hugo L. Black and Martin Luther King, Jr., George F. Kennan and Václav Havel, Harry S. Truman and Ralph J. Bunche, George Orwell and Edmund Wilson, and especially Thurgood Marshall.

Such idealistic heroes supply us with much of our moral substance. They remind us of what is possible; they are exemplars of the best that humankind can be and do—as Hamlet said, "how noble in reason! . . . in action how like an angel!" I remain convinced that it is possible to speak to "the better angels of our nature," to nurture the potential for idealism and commitment to service that is particularly pronounced in young men and women of college age.

The ultimate test of a liberal education ought to be its impact on the intellectual and moral lives of students. By the time they are graduated, students should feel that they have been exposed to an educational process of such transcending reach and transforming power that they have been challenged in every segment of their being. They should truly be able to say: "I am today a different person—a person more deeply aware of ambiguity, beauty, complexity, suffering, and truth than I was when I entered. My liberal education has changed me utterly."

(I would not argue, of course, that the qualities of mind and character that a liberal education seeks to develop can only be attained by attending a liberal arts college. Many men and women of meritorious achievement did not attend college at all, including five of this country's finest presidents—Washington, Jackson, Lincoln, Cleveland, and Truman—and some of the English language's greatest writers—Shakespeare, Jane Austen, Charles Dickens, Mark Twain, Henry James, Edith Wharton, George Bernard Shaw, Ernest Hemingway, Robert Frost, and Virginia Woolf. Men and women of such extraordinary capacities will always be exceptions to the rule.)

In the beginning and in the end, higher education is an experiment. Our nation has staked much on the success of that experiment. Whether it succeeds in the future, as it has in the past, will depend, finally, on our society's commitment to the values of liberal education.

This book derives in large part from essays I have written and speeches I have delivered, primarily at convocation and commencement exercises, over the past ten years. Most of the materials have been rewritten to cast them in essay form, to bring them up-to-date, and to achieve a greater unity among the several parts.

Prior publication of portions of the chapters of this book, or of earlier versions of them, has been as follows: "Introduction" appeared in the *Chronicle of Higher Education,* August 12, 1987; "Becoming an Educator" appeared in the *New York Times,* February 1, 1974; "A Dukedom Large Enough" appeared in *Harvard Magazine,* March–April 1992; "Presidential Prose" appeared in the *New York Times,* May 25, 1984; "The Promise of Equality" appeared in the *Hartford Courant,* January 15, 1990, in the *Los Angeles Times,* August 28, 1991, and in the *Boston Globe,* August 31, 1991; "The Organization of Knowledge" appeared in the *Chronicle of Higher Education,* November 18, 1987; "Science and Liberal Learning" appeared in the *Des Moines Register,* December 1, 1984, copyright 1984, the *Des Moines Register;* "Liberal Education and the Legal Profession" appeared in *Southwestern Law Journal* 39 (1985): 741 and in the *Los Angeles Times,* February 6, 1988; "The Lessons of the Law" appeared in *Iowa Law Review* 70 (1985): 487 (reprinted with permission) and *Iowa Law Review* 72 (1987): 1175 (reprinted with permission); "The Professor's Life" appeared in the *Chronicle of Higher Education,* February 19, 1986; "Thurgood Marshall: Man of Character" appeared in *Washington University Law Quarterly* 72 (1994): 1487, as well as in the *Boston Globe,* January 31, 1993, and January 24, 1994; "Originals and Copies" appeared in the *Atlanta Journal,* March 24, 1991; "Those Who Are Truly Great" appeared in the *Princeton Alumni Magazine,* February 19, 1992; and "Ordinary Backgrounds, Extraordinary Men" appeared in the *Boston Globe,* October 3, 1993. Several of the chapters appeared in the *Dartmouth Alumni Magazine* from 1987 to 1994. I am grateful to the editors of these publications for their assistance and to the publishers for their permission to reprint the relevant materials here. *George Kennan and the Dilemmas of U.S. Foreign Policy* by David Mayers (New York: Oxford University Press, 1988) was useful in the preparation of "Those Who Are Truly Great."

I am grateful for permission to quote from the following: *Making, Knowing and Judging* by W. H. Auden. Copyright © 1956, by permission of Oxford University Press. *Of Law and Men: Papers and Addresses of Felix Frankfurter.* Copyright © 1956 by Felix Frankfurter and renewed 1984 by Estelle Frankfurter and Philip Elman, reprinted by permission of Harcourt Brace & Company. *The Troubled Crusade: American Education 1945–1980* by Diane Ravitch. Copyright © 1983 by Diane Ravitch, reprinted by permission of HarperCollins Publishers, Inc. *The Collected Poems of Edwin Arlington Robinson* (New York: Macmillan, 1937), reprinted with permission of Simon & Schuster. *William Carlos Williams, Collected Poems 1939–1962,* vol. II, copyright © 1962 by William Carlos Williams, reprinted by permission of New Directions Pub. Corp. *Of Time and The River* by Thomas Wolfe. Copyright © 1935 Charles Scribner's Sons; copyright renewed © 1963 Paul Gitlin, Administrator, C.T.A., reprinted with permission of Scribner, an imprint of Simon & Schuster.

I am indebted especially to three colleagues for their editorial assistance: Mary Lynn Grant at the University of Iowa and Peter A. Gilbert and Edward Connery Lathem at Dartmouth. My friend Nardi Reeder Campion of Hanover read early drafts of many of the chapters in this book and provided encouragement at every stage of the way.

1. Life and Letters

Becoming an Educator

When I was a schoolboy, we were required to read Macaulay's magisterial *Essay on Johnson*. Published in 1856, it remains an ideal model of expository prose and one of the best short assessments of the life and work of the great eighteenth-century critic and lexicographer. The final homework assignment was to identify the sentence in Macaulay's essay that best captured the essence of Johnson's life. The memory of that essay has stayed with me ever since, as has the key sentence: "But the force of his mind overcame every impediment."

Few of us in this post-Freudian age are apt to believe that we can encapsulate the essence of our own life in a single sentence. But sometimes lives do seem to be framed by a theme. For me, the central theme has surely been a love of learning and reading, together with, from an early age, the profound desire to become a scholar and a teacher. Almost everything that I have sought to achieve, personally and professionally, derives from that theme.

A more difficult and interesting task is to identify the forces that created and shaped that defining theme. For me, as for most people, those forces were primarily family and education. As Pope wrote in his *Moral Essays*, "'Tis education forms the common mind, / Just as the twig is bent the tree's inclined." In my case, the twig was bent both by my father and by my mother, although each did so in quite different ways.

Born in London, my father came to this country when he was seven years old. At Bates College, from which he was graduated in 1920, he read widely in English and American literature, forming a particular admiration for Shakespeare, Emerson, Hawthorne, and Poe. However, as an immigrant to this country, he wanted to learn more about literature written by Jews, and he proposed, accordingly, to write a senior thesis on the novels of Israel Zangwill—books now long forgotten, books with such characteristic titles as *The Mantle of Elijah, Children of the Ghetto, Dreamers of the Ghetto*, and *The Melting Pot*. Although Zangwill was one of the most popular Jewish writers of the early years of this century (his collected works, published in 1925, run to fourteen volumes), my father's advisor did not regard Zangwill as an acceptable subject for a thesis. He urged my

9

father to select another—by which he undoubtedly meant a less provincial and more mainstream—writer.

My father next suggested Abraham Cahan, the founder of the influential Yiddish-language newspaper in New York City, the *Jewish Daily Forward*, and author of *The Rise of David Levinsky* and *The Imported Bridegroom and Other Stories of the New York Ghetto*, both of which he wrote in English. Although Cahan was admired by no less a literary figure than William Dean Howells for the realism with which he depicted ghetto and immigrant life, my father's advisor urged him to look still further for a topic. Although I do not know the outcome of my father's search for a thesis topic, the story is for me a poignant demonstration of the significance he placed on understanding those writers who sought to explore what it meant to be an immigrant Jew in America.

My father was a gentle, bookish man of extraordinary personal strength. Through his own reading habits, he set a powerful example. Indeed, in the most characteristic recollection I have of him, he is settled into a comfortable living room chair after dinner, as he was almost every evening, reading books worth reading. He was by profession a teacher of high school English, and he truly loved the classic works he taught: *Macbeth*, *Idylls of the King*, *The House of the Seven Gables*, *Ethan Frome*, *Silas Marner*, and *David Copperfield*. He is remembered to this day, by a generation of students, as an effective and caring teacher.

My mother, too, loved literature. Although her formal education extended only through high school, she was well read and numbered among her proudest possessions a handsome two-volume set of *The Life and Letters of Jean-Jacques Rousseau*, as well as several dozen of the original volumes of the Modern Library, including many of her favorites–*The Golden Treasury* and works by such writers as George Gissing, H. G. Wells, Anatole France, Olive Schreiner, Sherwood Anderson, Eugene O'Neill, Edith Wharton, W. H. Hudson, and James Branch Cabell.

Although my mother enjoyed literature, it was not the propelling force in her life that it was in my father's; for him, literature was virtually a way of life. The defining force in my mother's life was quite different: a powerful ambition for her son to succeed. She yearned to be identified with the Brahmin and Establishment figures that she read about in the *Boston Globe*—persons with venerable family names like Adams, Bradford, Cabot, Eliot, Lodge, Lowell, and Saltonstall.

Understandably, my mother resented our modest economic circumstances. Among my parents' circle of friends, she was the only wife who worked, as a bookkeeper at a local bank. She resented the fact that we never owned a home or a car, never took a vacation, and rented mostly second- and third-floor walk-up apartments. At some unconscious level, she must also have resented the elevated (and mostly inherited) social status of the Establishment figures whose lives she followed in the press, even as she envied that status. But her conviction, however unrealistic, that her life of deprivation could be redeemed by her son's achievements—that her sacrifices would be rendered worthwhile by my making a mark on the world—created a powerful pressure for me to succeed, and to do so, moreover, within clearly defined and socially endorsed contexts.

Profoundly insecure, my mother was driven, as I became driven, by what Virginia Woolf called "the pressure of convention." Whenever she was asked to inscribe the keepsake books of the children of family friends graduating from high school, she would usually write, "May you sail on the good ship Ambition, and land on the isle of Success." She wrote these words without any sense of irony or any hint of doubt that America might not always function as a meritocracy or that success sometimes might not be the inevitable outcome of ambition and hard work.

My mother truly expected me to become a major maker of national policy, in the model of one of her aristocratic heroes, like Franklin D. Roosevelt or Dean Acheson or Averell Harriman. The pressure of her ambition for me made me uncomfortable; sometimes it frightened me. I still have the copy of John Gunther's memoir of his son who died young, *Death Be Not Proud*, which she gave me when I was thirteen. It bears the disconcertingly somber inscription, "May you in a small way emulate the character and thoughtfulness of John Gunther, Jr." But while she was holding up to me the character and thoughtfulness of John Gunther, Jr., I saw him, first and foremost, as a young boy—only a few years older than I was—who had died. Her Edwardian notions of heroism, even unto martyrdom, were often more oppressive than inspiring.

Still, it was the force of her displaced resentment, projected ambition, and identification with cultural and social orthodoxy that motivated me to seek academic distinction, and that motivation was responsible for my attending the two academic institutions that so decisively shaped my desire to be a teacher and scholar—Harvard College and Yale Law School.

Although our home was not a deeply religious one, I now keenly appreciate the extent to which being Jewish also marked my growth as a young man. Being Jewish means many things to me, but none is more important to my identity than Judaism's tradition of scholarship and learning. Perhaps that is why I became a teacher, seeking to extend that tradition by following the Talmud's observation, "When you teach your son, you teach your son's son."

The mill city of Manchester, New Hampshire, where I was born and grew up, was "a little United Nations," as my father used to say, populated by old-line Yankees and persons with French-Canadian, Greek, Italian,

Lebanese, Armenian, and Polish roots. At Manchester Central High School, many of my classmates—like the characters in Derek Walcott's *Omeros*—had classical names, like Aphrodite, Apostolos, Aristides, Basilios, Menelaus, Persephone, Plato, Socrates, and Vasilike. My school years were an undeniably democratic experience. Growing up in such an American "melting pot," I often wondered what distinguished me from my classmates—in short, what it meant to be a Jew. I gradually came to understand that a serious devotion to learning was at the center of Jewish identity.

As an adolescent, I came to know every nook and cranny in Manchester's Carpenter Memorial Library, an elegantly proportioned marble palace that commanded an elevated position above Victory Park, in the center of Manchester's downtown section. Books were my sanctuary from the unsettling mysteries of adolescence, my refuge of quiet reflection from the confusions of an adult world in which I could not confide.

I came of age during the fifties, a decade that celebrated an orderly and bland domestic society that too often was racist, sexist, exclusionary, and indifferent to the claims of individualism; abortion, divorce, and civil rights were low on its political agenda. My introduction to a certain frivolous part of the cultural style of the fifties came when I saved baby-sitting and lawn-mowing dollars in order to make my first trip to New York City, alone, during the Christmas vacation of my senior year in high school. The primary purpose of the trip was to see four plays—*The Moon Is Blue* with Barbara Bel Geddes, *The Male Animal* with Elliott Nugent, *The Millionairess* with Katharine Hepburn, and (at a Christmas matinee) *Dial M for Murder* with Maurice Evans.

These plays hardly embodied a sense of *gravitas*, and today they seem hopelessly dated. The first two were witty spoofs of sexual mores in a more innocent age, the third was a typically Shavian example of the vigorous femininity that was soon to emerge in full force, and the last was a conventional, albeit elegant, drawing-room murder mystery. But as the first plays I ever saw on Broadway, they ignited a lifelong interest in the theater and have ever since seemed to me emblems of the lighter side of the fifties.

My parents encouraged reading and conversation about ideas; their pantheon was peopled with intellectuals, mostly Jewish, I noticed even then: Freud, Brandeis, Einstein, Frankfurter, Salk. And so, as I matured, my search for my authentic self was ineluctably linked to my identity as an intellectual, and that identity was inextricably linked to my sense of myself as a Jew.

For my parents, the choice of the college I would attend was of preeminent concern. They understood that academic achievement was the vehicle to a prominent station in American life. To their generation of New England Jews, Harvard represented the most exalted educational opportunity available and the most reliable vehicle of upward social mobility. Being a Harvard graduate was, to them, the next best attainable status to being a *Mayflower* descendant.

Fortunately the pressure on me in this respect was relieved by my acceptance into the Harvard class of 1957. And my experience as an undergraduate confirmed everything that my parents and my Jewish upbringing had inculcated in me about the joys of learning, even though Harvard then provided but a handful of Jewish faculty members who might serve as academic role models. Although I noticed the paucity of Jewish professors at Harvard, at the time it did not strike me as especially odd. Only later, when I entered Yale Law School, where nearly half the faculty was Jewish, did I meet Jewish professors whom I could emulate— most notably three who became lifelong friends, Alexander M. Bickel, Louis H. Pollak, and Joseph Goldstein.

I dearly wish that my father, who had confronted the harsh reality of anti-Semitism in finding his early teaching positions, had lived long enough to see the installation of Jewish presidents at numerous Ivy League and Big Ten universities during the 1980s and 1990s, when American society came of age in recognizing Jewish scholars as academic leaders.

The critic Alfred Kazin once observed that the distance between the International Ladies Garment Workers Union and the American Psychiatric Association is one generation. By pursuing scholarship and learning, American Jews of my generation have, indeed, bridged that distance, taught their children's children, and made their mark on American life— earning Nobel Prizes; writing novels now regarded as quintessentially American, rather than provincially Jewish (as the novels of Zangwill and Cahan had been regarded in my father's student days); analyzing economic and social trends, and discovering the secrets of the human mind and body.

Many memoirs of that period—the Eisenhower era—describe it as one of political passivity. And yet this was a period bursting with decidedly powerful ideas. As undergraduates who were coming of age intellectually, my friends and I wrestled intensely, often late into the night, with the encompassing claims of Freudianism, Marxism, existentialism, and Keynesianism.

We read books that would change forever how we thought about the world and ourselves—books with bold and synoptic themes, like Berlin's *The Hedgehog and the Fox*, Erikson's *Childhood and Society*, Freud's *The Interpretation of Dreams*, Frye's *Anatomy of Criticism*, Galbraith's *The Affluent Society*, Hofstadter's *The Age of Reform*, Matthiessen's *The*

Achievement of T. S. Eliot, Niebuhr's *The Children of Light and the Children of Darkness*, and White's *Social Thought in America*. These books, as well as many others of comparable originality, taught me the power of ideas, as a liberal education should.

We studied the political and historical analyses of Joseph Schumpeter, George F. Kennan, Reinhold Niebuhr, Richard Hofstadter, Louis Hartz, and Jean-Paul Sartre, and we devoured the novels of Lawrence, Conrad, Forster, Hemingway, Faulkner, Gide, Malraux, Camus, and Cozzens. We absorbed the poetry of Eliot, Yeats, Stevens, Auden, cummings, and Dylan Thomas, and we embraced the plays of Ibsen, Chekhov, Shaw, O'Casey, O'Neill, Williams, Miller, and Beckett.

We sat at the feet of outstanding literary critics: Douglas Bush, the great Miltonist; Walter Jackson Bate, the brilliant biographer of Johnson and Keats; Perry Miller, the seminal interpreter of the American Puritans, the New England Mind, and the transcendentalists; and Albert J. Guerard, the author of critical studies of Bridges, Conrad, Hardy, Gide, Dickens, and Dostoyevsky, and an early champion of the novels of his student John Hawkes.

We attended lectures by scholars of breathtaking learning: Arthur M. Schlesinger, Jr., the American intellectual historian who was as penetrating in discussing William Graham Sumner and Walter Rauschenbusch as he was shrewd in analyzing Andrew Jackson and Franklin D. Roosevelt; and Frederick Merk, a compelling lecturer who traced with an unsurpassed skill the westward movement and the spirit of manifest destiny.

My Harvard tutor, John V. Kelleher, seemed to know more about James Joyce than anyone else in the world. He inspired me to read more closely and more carefully than I ever had done before. His copies of *Ulysses* and *Finnegans Wake*, which he extensively annotated and interlined with his comments on those often-baffling texts, must have been documents of exceptional critical brilliance. And Dr. George A. Buttrick, who preached every Sunday morning in Memorial Church, beckoned me to reflect on the perplexing ironies (a favorite term of the fifties) of seeking to lead a moral life and to exult in the sublime glories of which the human soul was capable. (His sermons, later published in a book, *Sermons Preached in a University Church*, are as moving today as they were nearly forty years ago.)

For one who was fortunate to be an undergraduate at Harvard at the time, how could I accede to the conventional claim that these were years of intellectual and spiritual aridity? These books and these men (my professors were all men) made me want to be a reader, a teacher, a scholar, a learner for life. They inspired me—an anonymous student sitting in classes typically of several hundred—to be passionate about the life of the mind. I yearned to remain in the company of scholars; I hungered to write books like those I so admired from my classes. What could be more thrilling or ennobling, I thought—what could be worthier or more rewarding—than a career that made me a part of the academic enterprise?

As much as I thrived on the intellectual stimulation of Harvard, my performance as a student was not exceptional enough to capture anyone's attention, nor did it qualify me for membership in Phi Beta Kappa. I was ardent, steady, competent, and reliable, but never brilliant or creative. My fear of failure—of missing the opportunity to attain a secure place—was too great to allow that imaginative risk taking that brilliant students exhibit.

All this changed when I entered Yale Law School. Here was a professional school that taught law as one of the liberal arts. I admired everything about Yale: the brilliance of the faculty, the power of the Socratic method of teaching, the challenge of fashioning those wise restraints that make men and women free, the view of law as a policy science, the emphasis on legal education as a vehicle for the preparation of leaders. Best of all, Yale Law School was an authentic meritocracy. My classmate Alan M. Dershowitz expressed it well in his book *Chutzpah* when he wrote, "Though my fellow classmates numbered among them children of presidents, Supreme Court justices, and multimillionaire industrialists, the only hierarchy I ever saw at Yale Law School was based on grades, *Law Journal* writing, moot court competition, and classroom performance."

In an environment of such values, I flowered as a student, earning grades that were among the best in the class, and dreaming, during the magical days of John F. Kennedy's presidency, that all things were possible for a liberally educated lawyer. (My father, having watched so many high school students of indifferent performance become significant successes in later life, would have described me as a "late bloomer." Ironically, it may have been that the very pressure to conform that had directed me to Harvard was also one of the factors that had inhibited me from excelling there. Only after I had become more secure in myself intellectually—perhaps in the process of maturation that occurred when I took time off to work as a journalist between college and law school—did my academic achievement approach my aspirations.)

The three years during which I was a law student were years of great intellectual vitality. Scholars like Alexander M. Bickel, Paul A. Freund, Walter Gellhorn, H. L. A. Hart, Louis L. Jaffe, and Louis H. Pollak were at the height of their powers, and I can still recall the excitement with which I read four important books published during my student years: *The People and the Court* by Charles L. Black, Jr., *The Common Law Tradition* by Karl N. Llewellyn, *The Sovereign Prerogative* by Eugene V. Rostow, and *Principles, Politics, and Fundamental Law* by Herbert L. Wechsler. During these same years, Professor Bickel, whom I so greatly admired as a teacher and scholar, was completing his masterful essay, *The Least Dangerous Branch*, published soon after I graduated.

From the very start of my law school years, I was taken by the humane learning, not to say the heroic examples, of Learned Hand and Felix Frankfurter—great judges who appreciated that the law, properly understood, must be informed by the liberal arts. I was thrilled when I came across Judge Hand's statement:

> I venture to believe that it is as important to a judge called upon to pass on a question of constitutional law, to have at least a bowing acquaintance with Acton and Maitland, with Thucydides, Gibbon and Carlyle, with Homer, Dante, Shakespeare and Milton, with Machiavelli, Montaigne and Rabelais, with Plato, Bacon, Hume and Kant, as with the books which have been specifically written on the subject.

Similarly, I was charmed by Justice Frankfurter's response to a twelve-year-old boy who had written seeking advice as to how he might prepare himself for a career in the law:

> No one can be a truly competent lawyer unless he is a cultivated man. If I were you, I would forget all about any technical preparation for the law. The best way to prepare for the law is to come to the study of the law as a well-read person. Thus alone can one acquire the capacity to use the English language on paper and in speech and with the habits of clear thinking which only a truly liberal education can give. No less important for a lawyer is the cultivation of the imaginative faculties by reading poetry, seeing great paintings, in the original or in easily available reproductions, and listening to great music. Stock your mind with the deposit of much good reading, and widen and deepen your feelings by experiencing vicariously as much as possible the wonderful mysteries of the universe, and forget all about your future career.

For a law student who was passionately, even deliriously, caught up in the legal issues of the time—*Brown v. Board of Education* (1954), holding segregation in the public schools unconstitutional, had been decided only several years earlier; and *Baker v. Carr* (1962), opening the way for pronouncement of the one-person, one-vote requirement for legislative apportionment, was decided during my third year—it was difficult to find the time to pursue Hand's and Frankfurter's advice. But I do remember reading, on late evenings, several memorable books of the period, including *By Love Possessed* by James Gould Cozzens, *To Kill a Mockingbird* by Harper Lee, *A Death in the Family* by James Agee, *The Prime of Miss Jean Brodie* by Muriel Spark, *The Mansion* by William Faulkner, and Mark Schorer's biography of Sinclair Lewis, the author whose novels had converted me into a reader when I was fifteen.

One of the academic highlights of my years at Yale Law School was participating as a finalist in the moot court appellate competition. My partner and I did the very best we could, and we were pleased with our performance, but in the end the judges decided that the other team had won. (This outcome was a replay of my experience as a high school debater; my partner and I advanced to the state final argument all four years and lost each time.)

I went to sleep discouraged and woke up early the next morning to take a walk. As I walked the streets of New Haven, I met Justice John Marshall Harlan, a kindly man who had been the presiding judge the evening before. He was taking *his* early morning walk. We stopped to talk, and he told me that whenever he had lost an appellate argument during the years when he practiced law, he had summoned up two lines from Tennyson that his father had recited to him when he was a boy: "'Tis better to have loved and lost / Than never to have loved at all." At a moment of dejection, I had, ironically, found common ground with a Supreme Court justice!

In the year immediately following my graduation from law school, I had the privilege of serving as law clerk to Judge Thurgood Marshall, then a member of the United States Court of Appeals for the Second Circuit. In that year I learned from a great advocate that law must be practiced not only with craft and passion but also with a tenacious commitment to ideals. I learned from a moral man that the truly great among us are those who retain a generosity of spirit in the face of mean injustice. I learned from a master that a person at the end of a very long lever can move the world.

On the strength of my third-year seminar paper (published in the *Yale Law Journal* under the ungainly title "Prospective Overruling and Retroactive Application in the Federal Courts") and the recommendation of Judge Marshall, I was appointed in 1964, at age twenty-eight, to the faculty of the University of Pennsylvania Law School. With that appointment, my career in higher education began.

Penn was a wonderful place to enter upon a career as a law professor. Embedded in its culture was an historic sensitivity to one of the enduring questions that any law school faces: how to justify its place in a university committed to liberal learning. Almost a half-century before I began teaching, Thorstein Veblen, in his book *The Higher Learning in America*, had called attention to the possibility that professional education was inconsistent with the proper goals of a university. He warned that once professional schools, teaching marketplace skills, gained a place within a university, they would ultimately doom the pursuit of liberal learning. The question Veblen raised went to the very soul of legal education; it required that law schools, like other professional schools, justify their right to exist within a university setting.

Penn Law School did remarkably well in exemplifying that justification. It traced its founding to a series of lectures delivered in 1790 by James Wilson, a signer of the Declaration of Independence, one of the six original justices of the United States Supreme Court, and the preeminent legal scholar of his generation. Wilson raised a noble standard in stating, "Law and Liberty cannot rationally become objects of our love, unless they first become objects of our knowledge."

Penn truly believed that law was a mode of cultural explanation and social understanding. The faculty was devoted to teaching law and training lawyers in what Justice Holmes called "the grand manner"—a manner that regarded the law as sustaining and enriching civilization by asking searching questions about political and social values, by setting high aspirations for the achievement of fairness and justice, and by offering to students a vision of the largest possibilities that a life in the law offers for intellectual satisfaction, public service, and personal idealism.

In this stimulating environment, I spent my next eighteen years, teaching administrative law, family law, and torts. My specialty became administrative law, which concerns the rules that govern the decision-making processes of governmental officials and bureaucracies; these rules reflect the principles of procedural due process and fundamental fairness prescribed by the Constitution, as well as statutory requirements, the needs of effective administration, and the dictates of good sense.

These were years of personal contentment and professional growth. The law was, indeed, a "jealous mistress," but it rewarded the intense attention it demanded. From the very first class I taught—the case for discussion, *Ives v. South Buffalo Railroad Company* (1911), involved a challenge to one of the early workmen's compensation laws—until the very last, I enjoyed the thrust and parry of jousting intellectually with eager young minds. Today I take great pride in the fact that among my former students are federal and state court judges, law professors, and leading members of the bar. I also found satisfaction in the joys of creativity that came from scholarship, and over the years I published a book, *Crisis and Legitimacy: The Administrative Process and American Government* (1978), as well as many articles in law reviews and other publications.

My first venture into academic administration came in 1973, when I accepted an appointment as university ombudsman. Having spent nine years thinking and writing about problems related to the fair administration of governmental agencies, I could hardly turn down an opportunity to play a part in ensuring the fairness of the procedures by which the university reached its decisions and administered its policies.

It seemed to me, as something of a hypothesis as I set out on my duties, that in a university community the informal methods of an ombudsman held greater promise of protecting individuals from arbitrary administrative action than more formal methods did. The fact that formal methods of protecting individual rights (the most prominent being adversary hearings, with the right of confrontation and cross-examination) have traditionally been less developed in universities than in other social institutions, such as governmental agencies and courts, meant that there would be occasion for testing this hypothesis against a wide variety of situations.

Some of the complaints I received were the result of nothing more venal than administrative inadvertence or oversight, and a telephone call or a short personal discussion usually brought corrective action. Other complaints proved on investigation to be the result of an administrative failure to follow a governing rule or practice, and the persons responsible were generally quite ready to make effective amends when I was able to show that they had not, in Justice Holmes's famous phrase, "turned square corners" in dealing with the individual involved.

As part of my learning process, I came gradually to appreciate that the informality of an ombudsman's methods—the absence of publicity, the protection of individual identities, the use of a conciliatory rather than an adversarial approach—often held greater promise of achieving a just result than more formal methods do. Now, in a period in which more and more academic questions have become justiciable issues in courts of law, I worry that this lesson is being forgotten.

Serving as the university ombudsman brought me into poignant contact with some of the saddest of academic circumstances. I met many persons seeking help in meeting grave personal problems for which there were no ready solutions: faculty members who had been denied tenure and could not find new positions elsewhere; students with fine academic records who had surrendered to the temptation to cheat under the focused pressures of a moment and now had to find explanations for parents, friends, and graduate schools; secretaries who had served now-retired professors for the better part of a professional lifetime and could not find suitable new positions.

The hurt that I saw in such cases was extraordinarily great. These were people essentially pleading for an affirmation of their worth as human beings. The limited range of the responses that an ombudsman can make in such situations merely confirmed the intractability of their dilemmas. Often, the most that an ombudsman could do was to strive to ensure that the bureaucracy—like a physician—does no harm and, in its rigidity, does not add insult to injury. I concluded my service with a sense of satisfaction that, by demonstrating the value of informal methods of dispute resolution in a world that often seems to be hurtling toward an increasing reliance on adversary modes of adjudication, an ombudsman could help to humanize a university.

My experience as ombudsman, and later as associate provost of the university, enlarged my interest in university governance and academic administration. In 1979, I was appointed dean of the law school. For the next three years, I worked with the faculty to strengthen our educational program, especially in ways that emphasized the liberal education of lawyers. We enriched our offerings in international education by establishing exchange programs with universities in France, Great Britain, Israel, and Poland, and we deepened a commitment to interdisciplinary education by introducing into the curriculum greater components of the social sciences, especially city planning, economics, legal history, medicine, Middle East studies, political science, and public policy analysis.

Being dean of the Penn Law School also afforded me two significant opportunities for public service: as chair of the Pennsylvania Legislative Reapportionment Commission and as a member of the City of Philadelphia Board of Ethics. (In later years, I would be fortunate to receive other such opportunities, including service as chair of the Iowa Governor's Task Force on Foreign Languages and International Study and as a member of the board of the Jacob K. Javits Fellowship Program.)

No part of my deanship did more to develop my interest in administration than the opportunity to work closely with the university's president, Martin Meyerson, and its two successive provosts of that time, Eliot Stellar and Vartan Gregorian. From them I learned that able administrators who have established their standing as scholars and who exhibit a devotion to the highest values of academic life can have an unparalleled intellectual influence on an institution. By virtue of their position and their character, such academic leaders can be teachers of an entire community. I came to realize that the true importance of holding a senior administrative position was the power to enunciate the academy's central values and the responsibility to set forth the university's agenda (even if one did not always prevail in the subsequent discussion). It was this inspiring realization that turned my thoughts toward becoming a university president.

When, in 1982, the opportunity came to become president of the University of Iowa, I accepted enthusiastically. Having spent one summer, a decade earlier, teaching at the law school there, I had come to admire the university and to appreciate the civilized joys of Iowa City. My five years at Iowa, from 1982 to 1987, were a time of marked personal growth, during which I developed a vast increase in my understanding of higher education and an enhanced appreciation of public universities.

After my appointment, I asked several friends what I might profitably read to prepare myself for a job larger than any I had ever held. None was able to make a suggestion, although several sagely counseled that I learn the two most important phrases in a president's lexicon: "Thank you" and "I'm sorry." I have since found four books that I recommend to those who now ask the same question of me. Interestingly, the most instructive and delightful are not how-to-do-it manuals, and they were not written by presidents at all. Two are novels: *The Masters* by C. P. Snow and *A Friend in Power* by Carlos H. Baker. The other two are memoirs: *Where Has All the Ivy Gone?* by Muriel Beadle, wife of George W. Beadle, president of the University of Chicago; and *It's Different at Dartmouth* by Jean A. Kemeny, wife of my late predecessor, John G. Kemeny. These books are rich in insight and counsel, especially in their demonstration of the wisdom of maintaining a sense of humor, irony, and distance in discharging one's presidential duties.

Having been educated at Harvard and Yale and formed as a teacher and scholar at the University of Pennsylvania, I found the move from the East Coast and the Ivy League to the Midwest and the Big Ten remarkably instructive. There were, of course, some obvious differences. The cornfields of rural Iowa provided a more serene landscape than did the high-rise buildings and potholed superhighways of urban Philadelphia, and Iowa City provided an ease of daily life—by which I mean a freedom from the fear of crime and a ready access to parking—that Philadelphia could not match. But these differences—which my family and I considered advantages—were, in the larger perspective, small ones.

Much more significant was the vast intellectual breadth and human scale of a university of thirty thousand students, with professional schools in business administration, dentistry, education, engineering, law, medicine, nursing, and pharmacy, and with special schools in dental hygiene, journalism, religion, and social work. Here was a learning challenge writ large for someone whose formal academic ken had been no wider than a law school of seven hundred students, and I prospered intellectually from the daunting necessity to learn about so many fields of knowledge new to my experience.

Here, too, was an unmatched opportunity to observe the indispensable role that a public university plays in the life of a state—especially a rural state, where private higher education is less prevalent than in the East. Alumni of the University of Iowa are to be found in every part of the state and in every walk of life. Their years at the university inform who they are and what they do; they bind the state together in a shared experience, pride, and affiliation. It would be difficult to imagine the state of Iowa—with its need for well-educated accountants, businessmen and women, lawyers, nurses, pharmacists, physicians, and social workers—without the University of Iowa. Similarly, it would be difficult to imagine the delivery of superb health care in the state of Iowa without the university's 1,100-bed teaching hospital and its network of statewide health services. In short, the university was essential to the functioning of the state's public and private sectors.

From the very start, I was captivated by the students at Iowa. They were charming and wholesome, bright, and serious about their studies. Especially, I admired the grit and determination of those (perhaps a majority) who were pursuing a college degree under straitened family financial circumstances. For most, there had been little thought of attending any other university. Students in the top half of an Iowa high school class were entitled by law to attend the university, and most assumed from an early stage of their schooling that they would.

Most students entered the university from small-town farming communities and rural secondary schools, from families of hard work and modest means, from circumstances that gave them little experience in the larger world of foreign travel and limited exposure to the cosmopolitan world of art museums, symphony orchestras, and legitimate theater. Many of these students lacked the same "sense of destiny" as those from the more economically privileged and worldly families with whom I had previously been most familiar. The aspiration levels of Iowa's students often reflected an excessive modesty about their true intellectual capacities and a more circumscribed ambition for national stature—ambition that they were properly entitled to harbor.

Wondrously, all of this changed rapidly after they became immersed in their studies. The university, as it was classically intended to do, opened up whole new worlds to these students—worlds constituted by the works of Plato and Aristotle, Locke and Hume, Durkheim and Weber, Einstein and Whitehead, Shakespeare and Milton, Austen and Hardy. As it did so, the students grew in learning, in sophistication, and in aspiration.

I observed much of this progression firsthand by teaching an undergraduate course entitled "Private Lives and Public Institutions." Its reading list explored the crises of conscience that often confront individuals as they seek to define and understand their relationships with social institutions. In analyzing such rich and provocative material as *The Human Condition* by Hannah Arendt, *Reflections on the Revolution in France* by

Edmund Burke, *The Protestant Ethic and the Spirit of Capitalism* by Max Weber, *An Enemy of the People* by Henrik Ibsen, and *Billy Budd* by Herman Melville, the students and I found ourselves searching out, together, the meaning of human identity and the proper boundaries of conscience. The students were awakened to enduring issues of political theory, and for my part, I found the classroom a thoroughly exhilarating respite from the daily urgencies of academic administration—well worth the difficulty of arranging my schedule to accommodate the preparation and the class time involved.

When I am asked, as I frequently am, what the greatest difference is between the University of Iowa and the several other institutions I have known, I reply that it lies in the gratifying quantum of "value added" during the four years of an Iowa student's education. The phenomenon of "value added" is one important measure of the contribution that higher education makes to society. By arousing the latent talents of young men and women and by stimulating the most ambitious and productive uses of those talents, universities insure that human minds rich in promise will not (in a good Iowa phrase) lie fallow.

Still another difference between the three universities of my prior experience and the University of Iowa was, as I learned to my delight, Iowa's emphasis on the creative arts—writing, theater, dance, music, painting, printmaking, and sculpture. My initial skepticism about whether the creative arts were proper pursuits within a university—undergirded by Veblen's acid condemnation of their inclusion in college curricula— quickly gave way to a deep respect for their educational value.

Watching Paul Massey in the title role of *King Lear*, along with a cast of undergraduate students who had rehearsed with him for two months, was a vivid demonstration of the power of the performing arts to engage the intellect and imagination of the student participants. I became entirely persuaded, too, of the educational merit of enabling student playwrights, composers, and choreographers to see their work performed; the process refined and disciplined their talents and stoked their ambitions.

By engaging students in the vital process of seeking to create something beautiful that will inspire and endure, programs in the creative arts compel them to grapple—as all artists do—with what William Faulkner called "the problems of the human heart in conflict with itself." They become immersed, again in Faulkner's words, in the transcendent process of creating "out of the materials of the human spirit something that did not exist before."

The arts remain one of the surest means of conveying the lessons of a liberal education, uplifting the spirit, enlightening the soul, and schooling the heart and mind. Programs in the creative arts help students to achieve the fullness of human potential by instructing them in the fullness of human accomplishment.

Despite my enthusiasm for the arts within a liberal education, I came to regard certain aspects of specialized performing arts programs at colleges and universities as troubling. Because the "recruitment" of a prima ballerina or a mezzo soprano or a French hornist can be as essential to the success of an arts program as the recruitment of a quarterback for a football team, the pressure to compromise academic admissions standards can be as great in the one as in the other. Moreover, because we have entered an "age of virtuosity"—of near-professional preparation and competence—performing arts programs place heavy time demands on student musicians to maintain their skills by taking individual lessons, by practicing for long hours, and by attending rehearsals. These demands can entirely consume a student's life, just as participation in intercollegiate athletics also too often does.

Moreover, as students become more proficient and the level of their skills more professional, performing arts programs often tend to become more like conservatories and less like liberal arts departments. They encourage premature specialization, and their faculties too often press for separate schools of performing arts, oppose liberal arts core requirements (such as foreign languages, mathematics, and the sciences), and seek independent control over the admission of their students. These tendencies are troubling, especially at the undergraduate level, because they deny to students the full value of a liberal arts education.

The most eminent of the programs in the creative arts at Iowa is the Writers' Workshop, which was founded in 1936 and advanced into its second half-century during my tenure. Its graduates comprise a Who's Who of contemporary writers, including Wallace Stegner, Flannery O'Connor, William Stafford, Raymond Carver, John Irving, James Alan McPherson, Jane Smiley, T. Coraghessan Boyle, and Rita Dove. (Tennessee Williams was a graduate of the university, but not of the workshop.)

During many years of testifying before state legislative committees about the university's need for funds, I always expected to be asked, "In a period of financial constraints, how does the university justify using taxpayers' money to support the Writers' Workshop?" This never seemed to me a difficult question to answer. The university supported the Writers' Workshop because of the importance of what the workshop did. By educating its students to be better writers and readers, it contributed to the good of the State of Iowa and of the nation. A democracy needs perceptive writers, thoughtful readers, and reflective citizens whose lives are enriched by what they read and think. It needs these people just as surely as it needs lawyers and engineers and elementary school teachers. As William Carlos Williams wrote in his poem "Asphodel, That Greeny Flower":

It is difficult
to get the news from poems
yet men die miserably every day
for lack
of what is found there.

What writers do easily justifies a university's patronage of the writers themselves. A university is, after all, the patron of many sorts of professionals: astronomers, biologists, engineers, geologists, historians, lawyers, literary critics, physicians, psychologists. The university nurtures the work of such professionals by providing them with support, the colleagueship of accomplished peers, the stimulation of talented students, access to libraries and laboratories, and an environment in which their work is taken seriously. Creative writers deserve the same support.

So I vowed that if I ever had to face a legislative committee that questioned the university's support of the Writers' Workshop, I would make no apology. I would recall that Justice Holmes had once asserted, "Taxes are what we pay for civilized society." He was, of course, correct. The university applied people's taxes to maintain the Writers' Workshop because, in so doing, it advanced the prospects of a civilized society.

In 1987, after five years at the University of Iowa, I accepted an invitation to become president of Dartmouth College, thereby returning to the New Hampshire of my youth and to the Ivy League of my days as a student and law professor. Had my parents still been alive, they would have been very proud; they would have regarded this move to a prominent position in the establishment world of higher education as the apotheosis of their dreams. But they would have been wrong in assessing its primary import in my life. What it would have meant to them was not what it meant for me.

Matured by the experience I had gained at Iowa and more certain than ever of the value of a liberal education, I assumed my responsibilities at Dartmouth with a greater self-confidence than I had ever felt before. I was ready emotionally to be more bold in aspiration and less cautious in temper. It was, after all, for my judgment and values that the college's board of trustees had selected me as president. I was ready, for the first time in my professional life, to cast aside, where it was appropriate to do so, the crippling commands of convention and to be direct and unambiguous in articulating my views on issues of academic principle. The feeling was immensely liberating.

Fortunately, Dartmouth's trustees had given me a straightforward mandate: to strengthen the college academically, to make it a place of greater intellectual seriousness, and to help it shed certain of the stereotypes that clung to it. Among the more unfortunate stereotypes were that Dartmouth was male dominated, inhospitable to women, fraternity oriented, unintellectual, ultraconservative, and especially congenial for "jocks." An anonymous member of the board of trustees was widely quoted in the press as saying that my task was "to lift Dartmouth out of the sandbox."

In my inaugural address, which I realized would command greater attention than any subsequent speech I would give at Dartmouth, I spoke more boldly than I had ever done before. The speech, entitled "A Commonwealth of Liberal Learning," was a statement of my philosophy of liberal education; it was also a personal declaration of independence from the cautious and conventional manner that had limited my full effectiveness during my academic career, even as it had brought me to that podium.

In what I intended to be the most arresting and provocative passage in the speech, I proclaimed:

> We must strengthen our attraction for those singular students whose greatest pleasures may come not from the camaraderie of classmates but from the lonely acts of writing poetry or mastering the cello or solving mathematical riddles or translating Catullus. We must make Dartmouth a hospitable environment for students who march "to a different drummer"—for those creative loners and daring dreamers whose commitment to the intellectual and artistic life is so compelling that they appreciate, as Prospero reminded Shakespeare's audiences, that for certain persons a library is "dukedom large enough."

It was my judgment that such directness in speech would, in the long run, be the most effective means of advancing the vision that the trustees and I shared for the college. While some people were predictably offended by the plainness of my remarks, my comments captured the attention of the several audiences I was addressing. They provoked discussion, self-scrutiny, and consideration of fundamental issues of institutional purpose. Over time, the directness with which I initially set forth my vision has, I believe, served to move Dartmouth forward more effectively than more measured language would have done. Personal boldness, in short, bore institutional fruit.

In the months and years that followed, the college put into place a number of provisions designed to reemphasize Dartmouth's sense of academic purpose and to enable it more nearly to approach its full potential.

Through an aggressive admissions effort, we enlarged the proportion of women in the entering classes from 38 percent to parity, thereby changing the social dynamics of the classroom and of extracurricular life. We established a series of programs that permitted students to pursue original scholarship in collaboration with individual members of the faculty, thereby seeking to encourage students to take themselves seriously as scholars and also to consider pursuing graduate work in the arts and sciences. These programs included the Presidential Scholars Program, the Women in Science Project, the E. E. Just Program in the Sciences for Minority Undergraduate Students, and the Mellon Minority Academic Career Fellowship Program.

We redoubled our efforts in the recruitment of minority faculty members and students, although we faced the daunting disadvantage of being located in a rural, virtually all-white northern New England community. We established predoctoral fellowships for African-American, Native American, and Latino and Latina graduate students, so that we might do our part to increase the number of underrepresented minorities receiving doctoral degrees, as well as bring to the campus more persons from such backgrounds who might serve as mentors and role models for our minority undergraduate students. With the breaching of the Berlin Wall, we reached out to recruit students from Eastern Europe. We adopted new and more intellectually rigorous undergraduate degree requirements in the most significant revision of the curriculum in approximately seventy years.

We managed budgetary stringencies in a self-disciplined manner—and one premised on a commitment to maintaining need-blind admissions so that we could keep our doors open to every qualified student, regardless of his or her financial circumstances (a commitment that fewer than a dozen of our sister institutions are today able to sustain). Building on my experience at Iowa, we doubled the number of faculty members teaching creative writing, and we established a series of prose and poetry readings that brought to the campus such important writers as A. R. Ammons, Saul Bellow, Louise Glück, Grace Paley, Philip Roth, Mark Strand, Derek Walcott, and Richard Wilbur. These initiatives contributed to the robustness and richness of Dartmouth's intellectual life.

One attraction of coming to Dartmouth was that I expected a small college, with 4,200 undergraduates, to permit me the opportunity to be more directly in touch with students. However, the demands of administration and of the many other constituencies to which a president must relate—trustees, faculty, staff, alumni, fund-raisers, lawyers, government officials, and parents—proved greater than I had anticipated, and I soon found that I had to reserve specific time in my schedule in which to see students, if I did not want to be swamped by so many competing claims.

Accordingly, I hold open office hours for students—first-come, first-served—for an hour and a half every Monday afternoon, and I meet frequently with student groups. We discuss everything from the macro to the minute. These meetings have taught me much about what college students are thinking; they take me back to my own college days, reminding me of the identity crises and the soul-searching, self-absorbing preoccupations of late adolescence, of the painful struggles to find a balance between the present moment and the future, between the loud voices of society and the quiet call of one's inner self. They have reinforced for me the value of the intense intellectual passage, with all its attendant emotional and moral growth, that a liberal education guides. As I have come to know individual students well, I have taken pleasure in writing recommendations for graduate schools, Rhodes Scholarships, and fellowships to selection committees that, I suspect, rarely see letters from college presidents.

As president of Dartmouth, I have had many opportunities to speak to students—at public occasions like convocation and commencement ceremonies, at informal occasions in fraternity houses, and at honors dinners—and I have used these occasions to talk about my heroes and heroines and to recommend books that I admire. To my initial surprise, students have truly listened; often, students stop me on the street to remind me of something I said a year or two earlier—something that has stuck with them and caused them to think. Sometimes they have even returned the favor by recommending a book that they admire and believe I would enjoy.

I also have sought to place before students persons who are worthy exemplars of a liberal education, by selecting idealists, artists, and scholars as commencement speakers (the list includes Marian Wright Edelman, Joseph Brodsky, and Oscar Arias Sanchez) and as honorary degree recipients (among them Claire Bloom, Robert Coles, Rita Dove, John K. Fairbank, Helen Frankenthaler, Carlos Fuentes, Vartan Gregorian, Seamus Heaney, A. Leon Higginbotham, Jr., Jessye Norman, I. M. Pei, Jonas Salk, Robert M. Solow, Aleksandr Solzhenitsyn, Helen Vendler, Derek Walcott, and August Wilson).

In addition, every summer I send a letter to the members of the incoming freshman class. In it, I write, "As a Dartmouth student, you will have before you—in faculty and facilities—the best tools in the world with which to achieve a liberal education in order to enable you to become the person you wish to be. No endeavor, at this stage in your life, is more important. Your task, as St. Thomas Aquinas wrote, is 'to contemplate and bring to others the fruit of your contemplation.'"

In that letter, I add some words of advice for the remaining weeks before college actually begins:

First, devote a quiet hour or two to setting down—perhaps in the form of a letter to yourself—the reasons why you are coming to Dartmouth, the goals you hope to accomplish at college, and the values and aspirations that matter most to you as you begin this four-year segment of your life. These personal reflections, memorialized in writing for your later review, may, in the months and years to come, serve as a fixed point against which to measure your growth and accomplishments—or perhaps a signpost to put you back on course.

Second, read as much as you can. Make it a practice, particularly when you are not in the midst of course work, of always being in the midst of reading at least one or two good books. After all, if you haven't started a book, you are less likely to use a spare hour or evening in reading. Many of the books that I read as a college student have mattered to me ever since. I think, for example, of *Invisible Man* by Ralph Ellison, one of the finest American novels since World War II; *A Good Man is Hard to Find* by Flannery O'Connor, a brilliant book of short stories by a remarkable woman who lived her entire life in Milledgeville, Georgia; and *The Plague* by Albert Camus, a powerful allegory that considers the metaphysical dilemmas of evil and human suffering.

I think, too, of books I read in later years, such as *A Yellow Raft in Blue Water* by Michael Dorris, a moving coming-of-age novel of Native American life; *John Keats* by Walter Jackson Bate, a brilliant biography that depicts that youthful poet's extraordinary personal growth; *The Children of Light and the Children of Darkness* by Reinhold Niebuhr, a dispassionate consideration of the relationship between human nature and democratic culture; and *The Call of Stories* by Robert Coles, a collection of thoughtful essays that explore the humane connection between teaching and the moral imagination.

I have found the role of college president as teacher and mentor to be a splendidly satisfying one. I have taken pleasure in stressing to young and inquiring minds that a liberal education is the best foundation for a life of achievement, reflection, and idealism. And I have especially been heartened on all of those occasions when I have seen evidence that students have heard and embraced my message.

Now, in middle age, I look back on a life formed by many forces: the gentle learning of my father; the powerful ambition of my mother; the Jewish values of my youth; the stimulating academic environment of Harvard College, of Yale Law School, and of the University of Pennsylvania Law School; and the lessons I have learned while leading a great public university and a distinguished private college. These are the forces that have shaped, in fullest measure, my destiny as an educator.

Having participated in a geographical and intellectual odyssey from the East to the Midwest and back to the East again, I find, to my surprise, that I now have lived more than half my life in the New England state in which I was born. And, from the age of eighteen, I have spent virtually my entire life in academe, a circumstance that has awakened me to the most deeply held conviction of my professional life—the value of a liberal education—and has enabled me, through the mysterious processes by which human beings grow, to move from a youthful caution and prudence to a more mature confidence and directness, in ways that have strengthened my effectiveness, personally and professionally. I have learned what Robert Frost, New Hampshire's most distinguished poet, meant when he wrote, "the utmost reward / Of daring should be still to dare."

Has academe sometimes disappointed me? Of course it has. Academe is subject to all of the faddishness and meanness, the pettiness and pomposity, and the meretricious displays of vanity as is the rest of society. But surely I have disappointed academe from time to time as well. At its best, however—and that has been most of the time—academe has enabled me to make what has been, I trust, a good and thoughtful life.

The Joys of Collecting Books

I want to describe a passion of my private life—book collecting: how I started to collect books and why I continue to do so; what kind of collection I have and how I acquired it; and why the collecting of books is for me so satisfying an endeavor.

I have been fortunate, from a book-collecting point of view, in that I have moved twice in recent years, first from Philadelphia to Iowa City, and then from Iowa City to Hanover. On both occasions, the exigencies of moving caused me to rid my library of those books I no longer especially wanted. Identifying books as candidates for triage is not a congenial enterprise, but the fact is that some titles, with the passage of time, do come to seem less auspicious choices or, at least, less essential or interesting or charming than they once did.

I sometimes think in this connection of Thoreau, one of whose earliest books was *A Week on the Concord and Merrimack Rivers.* One thousand copies were printed. Several years later, his publisher, who needed the space in his warehouse, told Thoreau that there were 706 copies left. Thoreau asked that those 706 volumes be sent to him. Then he wrote in his journal, "I now have a library of nearly nine hundred volumes, over seven hundred of which I wrote myself." Well, I now have a library of forty-five hundred volumes, *one* of which I wrote myself!

My collecting habits have been open-ended, and my collection, therefore, does not have the overall coherence that many others do. It does not focus on a single author or a single genre or a single subject. Rather, it reflects a variety of interests, many of them identified with particular periods in my life. I have concentrated especially on American history, literary and political biography, social and literary essays, and twentieth-century fiction and poetry.

Among the writers best represented are some of those whom I admire most: Camus, T. S. Eliot, Faulkner, E. M. Forster, Gide, Günter Grass, Graham Greene, Hemingway, Robert Lowell, Mann, Robert Penn Warren, and Edmund Wilson. I also confess—because no book collector would be entirely credible if he or she did not—that I enjoy collecting books by that engaging pair of eighteenth-century friends, Boswell and

Johnson. Among the statesmen and jurists best represented are Jefferson, Lincoln, the two Roosevelts, John Marshall, and Justices Brandeis and Holmes.

Sometimes I wish that my collecting habits were less eclectic, so that my library would have a greater focus. In surveying the variety of my collection, I think of the remarks that Cyrus King of Massachusetts made in the House of Representatives, in 1814, during the debate over whether the United States should acquire Thomas Jefferson's library. "The bill," he said, "would put $23,900 into Jefferson's pocket for about 6,000 books, good, bad, and indifferent, old, new, and worthless, in languages which many cannot read, and most ought not."

There is a wonderful novel—as good as anything I know of on the passion of collecting—entitled *The Connoisseur* by Evan S. Connell, Jr. The central figure is a life insurance executive from New York who has recently, in middle age, become a widower. He is sad and lonely. One day his business responsibilities bring him to New Mexico. Having arrived a day early, he rents a car and drives to Taos. He stops at a shop where he sees a beautiful Mexican artifact from the Mayan period, a terra-cotta statue of a magistrate, seated with his legs crossed and his arms folded, five centuries old. He knows immediately that he must buy it:

> I want this arrogant little personage, he thinks with sudden passion. But why? Does he remind me of myself? Or is there something universal in his attitude? Well, it doesn't matter. He's coming home with me.

He becomes more and more fascinated by pre-Columbian artifacts, awed by their classic form and dignified beauty. They become precious to him, even though they had seemed valueless just before he visited Taos. He cannot understand the sense of obsession that is growing within him. He begins to experience a "mysterious excitement" and to appreciate, as a friend tells him, that "you can get hooked on this stuff." He visits dealers in New York, borrows library books by "properly accredited mandarins," and purchases a professional, stainless-steel jeweler's glass, with lenses that swivel in and out. He thinks to himself:

> Why is it that nothing except pre-Columbian art seems to matter much anymore? . . . I can't distinguish reality any longer. I'm gripped by an obsession. I suppose I should be alarmed, but as a matter of fact I am not. This is really rather pleasant. I want more. Do they all plead for more? And if they do, how does it end?

The Connoisseur is the best book I know on the passion of collecting—the unfathomable, irresistible urge to build a collection that aspires to completeness and wholeness.

Why is it that some people are collectors and others are not? Why is it that some people collect books, while others collect postage stamps, and still others collect autographs or silver coins or Toby mugs or paperweights or Wedgewood dishes or antique cars? Even young children are collectors, some of baseball cards, others of seashells and colored stones.

It is difficult to explain why collecting books—or any other objects—is so deeply satisfying. Many books are, to be sure, beautiful objects in and of themselves (although most are not), and owning beautiful objects is undeniably satisfying. But there is more to the appeal of books than that. Books can tell stories that possess a life of their own, and by possessing the book a collector may come near to feeling that he possesses that life.

And like many other collectible objects, books carry us backward in time and establish an imaginative bond with earlier periods. In so doing, they remind us of the most fundamental of human concerns: the continuity of humanity and the mortality of individuals. For these and other reasons not readily fathomed, collecting books is an avocation satisfying enough to sustain a lifetime.

No one can collect books without regular access to good bookstores. I have been fortunate in having lived most of my adult life in communities with good bookstores, new and secondhand—communities where I could collect books easily and enjoy the company of fellow book lovers. Those communities, starting with my college days, have been Cambridge, New Haven, New York, Philadelphia, Iowa City, and Hanover.

Justice Holmes once remarked that the law is a jealous mistress. The bookstore, too, is a jealous mistress. Mail-order catalogs, especially from private dealers with specialized offerings, are important, but nothing whets a collector's appetite so powerfully as a bookstore—and perhaps especially a secondhand bookstore. There a collector can experience the ecstasy of discovery. There a collector can appreciate a volume's binding and design, blow off a decade's accumulation of dust, and enjoy the feel of uncut pages beneath his thumb.

I have a clear recollection of when I started collecting books. It was in July 1950, during the summer after my freshman year in high school. My parents had quite properly required that I get a job that summer and begin to earn some money for college. I found a job washing dishes at the Elliot Hospital in Manchester, the New Hampshire city in which I grew up. The problem with washing dishes in a hospital kitchen, as I quickly learned, is that you must be at the hospital at six in the morning, to do the breakfast dishes, and you cannot leave until seven in the evening, when the last dish from dinner has been done.

Washing dishes was, I found, exhausting and boring. The residential neighborhood around the hospital provided nothing for me to do during the long hours between meals. I dearly wanted to quit. Eventually, I discussed my unhappiness with my father, who was a high school teacher of English, and who was keenly aware that I had yet to read a book on my own outside of a class requirement—not a single book. Sympathetic to my complaint, he allowed me to quit, but with the shrewd condition that I spend the rest of that summer doing some reading.

And so I went with my father to a charming bookstore in Manchester, the Book Nook, and bought the volume that was to start my adult life as a reader and to become the first book in my library, *Arrowsmith* by Sinclair Lewis. I still have that very copy, a Modern Library edition, and it still has its blue-and-black dust jacket—with a scientist in a white coat, sitting before a microscope—that seemed so classically stylized even forty years ago.

Once I sat down to read, I found *Arrowsmith* simply wonderful. How did Sinclair Lewis, the son of a small-town doctor, know so much? I went from *Arrowsmith* to *Main Street* and from *Main Street* to *Babbitt* and from *Babbitt* to *Elmer Gantry*—discovering in Lewis's work an America I had not seen, appreciating a dry and ironic style I had not previously sought to know.

Next I discovered W. Somerset Maugham. Although *Of Human Bondage, The Moon and Sixpence*, and *Cakes and Ale* may not be among the greatest novels of the twentieth century, these books drew me into the novelist's special realm and helped me to experience what fluent storytellers can achieve. Soon I was reading Maugham's urbane short stories about wealthy, elegant people exchanging witty remarks in the drawing rooms of London, as well as the more somber ones about desperate, lonely people living out their days in the Southeast Asian outposts of the British Empire.

For as long as I continue to love books, it will ever be Lewis and Maugham whom I recall most fondly, because they first excited my literary imagination and—most blessed of all—whetted my appetite to read more.

I remember another book, Kressman Taylor's *Address Unknown*, a tiny book that caused a sensation when it was published in 1938. A chilling story of betrayal and revenge, it consists of an exchange of letters, beginning in 1932, between an American businessman who is Jewish and a German friend in Munich. Concerned over developments in Germany, the American queries his friend about "this Adolf Hitler." "A black foreboding," he writes, "has taken possession of me." The German responds that under Nazi leadership, Germany is on the road to recovering its national greatness. With each letter his anti-Semitism and his enthusiasm for Hitler grow.

The German finds himself in deeper trouble with the authorities with the arrival of each letter from his friend. He begs the American to stop writing, lest his letters incriminate him further. The American agrees to stop writing, then writes again to implore his friend to take care of his daughter, who is traveling in Germany. The German responds that the daughter is dead, killed by storm troopers after he turned her away from his door. Despite his friend's urgent pleas to stop, the American's letters continue until his final letter is returned, stamped "Address Unknown."

Still another book that I read during my high school years, just weeks after it was published in 1951, was *The Catcher in the Rye* by J. D. Salinger, with its arresting opening lines, heralding a fresh style in American writing: "If you really want to hear about it, the first thing you'll probably want to know is where I was born, and what my lousy childhood was like, and how my parents were occupied and all before they had me, and all that David Copperfield kind of crap."

I wish I had the literary skill to convey fully the power that *The Catcher in the Rye* had for a reader who was precisely the age of Holden Caulfield. Here was a book that persuaded a teenage reader that there was at least one other person in this world who knew what it was like to experience the confusion and awkwardness of adolescence, to be awakened to the fraudulent hypocrisy of the world of adults. It was startling to discover an adult who appreciated the painful passage of adolescence. My parents seemingly did not—as far as I could tell, no one's parents did—and I had not met any other adult who did, either.

By now I was smitten by the power of the written word—the power to reveal, to elevate, to startle, to comfort, to entertain, to teach. I knew what Thornton Wilder meant when he wrote to a friend:

> If Queen Elizabeth or Frederick the Great or Ernest Hemingway were to read their biographies, they would exclaim, "Ah—my secret is still safe." But if Natasha Rostov were to read *War and Peace*, she would cry out as she covered her face with her hands, "How did he know? How did he know?"

And so, having been smitten by the power of the written word, I wanted to possess books.

The Modern Library editions, with which I started my library, were then priced at ninety-five cents; eventually they went up to a dollar twenty-five and, then, to a dollar sixty-five. They ranged from the classics to contemporary works, from *The Red and the Black* to *What Makes Sammy Run?* from *Crime and Punishment* to *All the King's Men.* My collection of Modern Libraries grew, and I now own more than one hundred, many dating back more than forty years.

When I was a junior in high school, I joined the Book-of-the-Month Club, and some of the money I earned during my last two years of high school went to buy those books that are now the oldest titles in my library—books like *John Adams and the American Revolution* by Catherine Drinker Bowen and Edgar Johnson's two-volume biography (in a solemn and dignified gray dust jacket) of Charles Dickens.

At Harvard, I majored in English literature and decided to buy only hardback editions of the books that were required for my courses. As I look at my library today, I recognize that as an important decision, because it led me to acquire permanent editions of Faulkner, Hemingway, Camus, Gide, Sartre, Mann, Forster, Woolf, Conrad, Lawrence, Shaw, Lowry, and many other authors whose work, available in hardback at the time, has long since been unavailable in cloth editions.

One of the many important opportunities that college offers is that of being in the presence of writers. Most colleges invite many writers to give readings from their works, and these readings serve to create a special experience—a sense of connection—between students and authors. Also, they often lead students to buy the writers' books—perhaps even, in an act at once of homage and of self-definition, to ask the authors to inscribe them.

During my undergraduate years, I had many opportunities to hear poets and novelists read. The occasion I remember most indelibly was a reading in 1955 by T. S. Eliot, who appeared on that occasion under the auspices of the *Advocate*, Harvard's literary magazine. I had competed unsuccessfully for membership on the *Advocate*, and I felt a special sense of yearning as I sat in Sanders Theatre that evening, a desire to identify with this Harvard graduate whose poetry and criticism dominated the consciousness of most undergraduates majoring in English. The author of *The Waste Land* and *Four Quartets*, Eliot was perhaps the most significant living poet and critic in the intellectual lives of undergraduates.

He was introduced by Archibald MacLeish, poet, playwright, and Harvard professor, who described meeting Eliot in the 1920s while both were young men in Paris. When Eliot got up, he said that, before he read his poetry, he wanted to speak a word of homage to Douglas Bush, an eminent Renaissance scholar on the Harvard faculty. Eliot had written a number of early essays downgrading Milton's stature as an English poet; it was Donne and the metaphysical poets, he had argued, who were the major poets of England immediately after Shakespeare. On that evening, however, Eliot announced that Professor Bush had persuaded him that Milton must indeed be ranked among the great English poets. Here was T. S. Eliot confessing to a critical mistake. His confession of error was an epiphany. For a stunning moment, it brought the audience into the intimacy of a writer secure enough, generous enough, to admit his judgment's fallibility.

In later years, while I was at the University of Iowa, I frequently had the pleasure of meeting writers who visited the Writers' Workshop. Over the course of several years, I had dinner with writers like John Hawkes, Czeslaw Milosz, Angus Wilson, Robert Coles, and John Irving. When people ask me teasingly, as sometimes they do, why I choose to put up with the slings and arrows that a college president must endure, I explain to them that one *does* get to meet the most interesting writers!

Indeed, one gets to meet not only authors who are well established but also the most promising younger writers as well. One of my greatest thrills at the University of Iowa was the regular opportunity that was afforded me to attend readings by graduates of the Writers' Workshop, young men and women whom the faculty regarded as having special promise. There is a special joy in knowing writers during the formative years in which their work is developing and their experience is deepening. By nurturing the talent of these writers, colleges and universities perform a valuable public service.

In collecting books, one comes to look on certain books as particular favorites. Sometimes they are special because of what they contribute to one's intellectual development or because of the circumstances or events associated with the time of one's first reading them. Sometimes they are special, too, because of their aesthetic impact as physical objects—the quality of their binding or design or paper or illustrations. But most often they are special because of the rareness of the truth in the intellectual and emotional chord that they strike.

There are any number of useful ways to characterize such special books. The *American Scholar* has hit on one. In 1955 and again in 1970, it invited a number of distinguished individuals to name what was in their judgment the most undeservedly neglected book that had been published during the last twenty-five years. (The first time, only one title was mentioned by more than one respondent, Henry Roth's *Call It Sleep*. It was subsequently reissued in paperback and discovered by a new generation of readers.)

Over the years, I have compiled my own list of undeservedly neglected books—books that have been important in my life, but which somehow have not retained the attention or fashionable regard of the critics; books that have not received the continuing recognition among common readers that I believe they deserve.

One of the books on my list is Nathanael West's novel *Miss Lonelyhearts*. West wrote only four books before he died, in an automobile accident, at the age of thirty-six. He is not well known today. Yet *Miss Lonelyhearts* is an important book, about a newspaperman who conducts an advice-to-the-lovelorn column. As he comes to appreciate that the letters he receives have been written by desperate people who have no one else to turn to for solace, he is drawn into the pathos of their fates and is destroyed finally by this involvement. For all its brevity, *Miss Lonelyhearts* is a rare American novel in the somberness of its pessimism and the savagery of its psychological insight.

Another book on my list of undeservedly neglected works is *When Memory Comes* by Saul Friedländer, an historian who teaches at Tel Aviv University and at the University of Geneva. The book begins with a haunting sentence: "I was born in Prague at the worst possible moment, four months before Hitler came to power." Friedländer's parents fled Czechoslovakia when he was seven and placed him in a Catholic seminary in France, which undertook to prepare him for the priesthood. However, as World War II is ending and Liberation comes, the young man who is Friedländer discovers his identity—that he is the child of Jewish parents—and passes through a profound intellectual and emotional crisis. Abandoning his Catholic vocation, he stows away on a ship bound for the newborn land of Israel, and there he begins a new life. I know few autobiographies so rich in insight, so filled with moral searching, so honest and effective in describing the dilemmas of adolescence.

Another book, similar in its theme, is *Stop-time* by Frank Conroy, a delicate memoir of a young man's coming of age. Like *When Memory Comes*, it begins with a poignant sentence: "My father stopped living with us when I was three or four." Conroy describes the experiences that all adolescents must grapple with as they grow toward maturity—family conflict, friendship, love, and sexual awakening. It is simply one of the best books of its kind that I know. (I might add, as a personal note, that many years after reading *Stop-time*, I had the pleasure of appointing Frank Conroy to be the director of the Writers' Workshop at the University of Iowa.)

There is still another book I wish were more generally appreciated, a book that I read as a college freshman, *The Plague* by Albert Camus. It is a powerful allegory about an epidemic of bubonic plague that afflicts the Algerian city of Oran. The central character is a physician who fights the plague and who thereby confronts the metaphysical dilemmas of evil and human suffering. *The Plague* addresses the most profound questions of human existence. How can one person find meaning in combating an unexplained evil so much larger than he can possibly cope with? How can he ascertain the moral worth of his efforts when the task is so daunting, so overwhelming—and, in Camus' word, so absurd?

Camus was a major figure in the intellectual lives of those of us who came of age in the 1950s. His novels, such as *The Stranger* and *The Fall*, and his essays, such as "The Myth of Sisyphus" and *The Rebel*, set forth a statement of existentialism that speaks directly to man's condition of isolation and estrangement in an indifferent universe. More than perhaps any other contemporary writer, Camus guided my generation of undergraduates in the exploration of the problem of evil and moral choice. Although *The Plague* occasionally appears on college reading lists, it is still too little known or read today.

Another unjustly neglected book, I believe, is *The Last Hurrah*, Edwin O'Connor's witty and charming novel about Frank Skeffington and his final campaign for reelection as mayor of Boston. As anyone who has read the book knows, it is in fact about the redoubtable James Michael Curley and the rough and tumble of Boston politics in the 1920s and 1930s.

When *The Last Hurrah* was first published, Mayor Curley insisted that it was not about him and that, indeed, he did not have any idea on whom Frank Skeffington was based. But as the book drew more and more admiration, as more and more readers embraced Frank Skeffington with affection, Curley began to soften. In a speech at the University of New Hampshire, some months after the book was published, Curley finally did concede his secret gratification that the book just might be a celebration of his career. Summoning all of his roguish charm, he related an account of an incident that occurred when he was governor of Massachusetts. Curley had walked into the marble halls of the State House on Beacon Hill in Boston and found cleaning women scrubbing the floors. Instructing them to get up, he said, "The only time a woman should be on her knees is when she is praying to Almighty God." As he told this story, Curley confirmed the veracity in life of what Edwin O'Connor had captured in art.

Had we but world enough and time, I could extend my list of undeservedly neglected books by many titles—especially some from more recent years. The list would include such books as *A Death in the Family* by James Agee, *Hue and Cry* by James Alan McPherson, *Heat and Dust* by Ruth Prawer Jhabvala, and *A Good Man Is Hard to Find* by Flannery O'Connor.

The point, I hope, is clear. Books earn their claim on our lives by their power to help us to think, to care, and to acquire standards of judgment and appreciation. Many books—surely vastly more than the limited number that currently appear on lists of "great books"—have the capacity to achieve these purposes. Each generation of readers and students identifies those books that especially appeal to its needs and concerns.

That is why the content of even the most traditional of "great books" lists has changed so considerably during the past century. That is why we need to think of literature in ways that are more inclusive, rather than less so. We need to seek the breadth of embrace that Mark Twain intended when he replied to a request that he suggest a book list. "Any book list is a good one," he said, "which does not include *The Vicar of Wakefield*."

Books like those I have mentioned–*Miss Lonelyhearts, When Memory Comes, Stop-time, The Plague,* and *The Last Hurrah*—are not likely to find their way onto a traditional "great books" list. Yet these are important, revelatory, and transporting books. They spoke to me when I first read them, most as a young man, and I have no doubt that they would speak to students today, in ways that are useful to their intellectual, moral, and emotional development.

Like many book collectors, I keep, in my wallet, a list of titles that I want to acquire. My current list, worn thin from being carried for so many years, has three dozen titles on it. Some, like Gore Vidal's *The City and the Pillar* and Graham Greene's *Brighton Rock*, have been on the list for twenty-five years. Others, like Gabriel Garcia Marquez's *Leaf Storm*, are more recent additions. I could kick myself for not having bought them when they first appeared. And so, whenever I go to a distant city and have an extra couple of hours, I search out its secondhand bookstores, hunting for those elusive volumes that will round out my collection.

As I do so, I continue to ask myself why I have found collecting books to be such a satisfying—indeed, irresistible—activity for so many years. Recently that question has led me to think hard about a passage in Tom Stoppard's play *The Real Thing*. Stoppard's protagonist, a marvelously articulate architect named Henry, proclaims his respect for words, and he defends them against the debasement of careless usage:

> Words don't deserve that kind of malarkey. They're innocent, neutral, precise, standing for this, describing that, meaning the other, so if you look after them, you can build bridges across incomprehension and chaos. But when they get their corners knocked off, they're no good any more. . . . I don't think writers are sacred, but words are. They deserve respect. If you get the right ones in the right order, you can nudge the world a little or make a poem which children will speak for you when you're dead.

Words do indeed deserve respect. Writers who get the right words in the right order really do "nudge" the world a little bit. And the best of those writers create works that will speak for them long after they are dead.

For me, the pleasure of collecting books rests, in the end, on the pleasure of possessing those works that speak across the generations and that succeed in enriching our lives by revealing to us the nature of the human condition.

A Dukedom Large Enough

As one who loves and collects books, I was honored several years ago to be asked to speak at a university that had just added the two-millionth volume to its library. It had selected the Second Folio edition of William Shakespeare to mark this special occasion. Shakespeare remains our greatest maker of books, our supreme exemplar of poetic achievement, our most luminous symbol of the capacity of language to capture for all time the dilemmas of the human condition and the triumphs and anguish of the human spirit.

It is a measure of Shakespeare's genius that even though he wrote primarily for the stage, we regard his work as the foremost *literary* achievement of our culture. When an unfettered imagination meets a work of Shakespearean literature, a miraculous transformation occurs. Those Elizabethan scripts, now almost four hundred years old, are quickened and virtually reenacted before the mind's eye.

The university at which I spoke had an especially handsome building to house its collection. And yet, as impressive and essential as bricks and mortar inevitably are, I was reminded on that occasion of the remarks of a university librarian at the dedication of a new library building on his campus. He told the audience assembled on the lawn before that structure, "This is not the library. The library is inside." The librarian was, of course, right. It is finally the collection of books—the *libris*—that constitutes the true substance and authentic strength of a university library.

When we celebrate a university's acquisition of its two-millionth volume, we also celebrate those who undertake the daunting task of writing books. The Book of Ecclesiastes was most assuredly right in asserting that "of making many books there is no end." By sheer virtue of the size of their holdings—their marathons of shelf space and the bulk of their catalogs—libraries intimidate those prospective authors who contemplate the writing of a book.

In the face of a collection of two million books, who would be presumptuous enough to believe that he or she could add to the world's store of truly original knowledge? Who would be confident enough to think that he or she could command the attention of discriminating readers? Who would be bold enough to doubt Samuel Johnson's pronouncement that libraries are monuments to "the vanity of human wishes"?

And yet tens of thousands of men and women undertake each year to write books, some doubtless motivated by vanity and others surely by professional obligation, but most by the simple desire to share their thoughts and work with others. They undertake to write books even though they recognize, as Huckleberry Finn did, that writing a book can be agony. "If I'd 'a' knowed what a trouble it was to make a book," Huck said, "I wouldn't 'a' tackled it, and ain't a-going to no more."

Not only is writing a book exceedingly hard work, but the risks of disappointment at the conclusion of the enterprise are considerable. No matter how brilliant or imaginative or charming a book may be, there is no guarantee that it will receive the response it deserves. Because the process of historical judgment on books is, sadly, a kind of natural selection—uneven, ragged, indifferent to originality, resistant to idiosyncrasy—many authors of worthy books never receive full or proper recognition.

Consider, for example, the chagrin of rejection that the historian Edward Gibbon must have felt when he presented the second volume of his great work, *The History of the Decline and Fall of the Roman Empire*, to the Duke of Gloucester. The duke examined the volume and said, "Another damn'd thick, square book! Always scribble, scribble, scribble! Eh! Mr. Gibbon?"

We regularly misjudge the quality of books, particularly those of our contemporaries. Among the authors who never received the Nobel Prize for Literature are Chekhov, Tolstoy, Twain, Proust, Conrad, Joyce, Auden, Frost, and Nabokov—names that are themselves an honor roll of literary distinction. During the decades in which these authors were passed over, the Nobel Prize was awarded to, among others, Rudolf Christoph Eucken, Paul Johann Ludwig von Heyse, Carl Friedrich George Spitteler, Henrik Pontoppidan, Jacinto Benavente, Grazia Deledda, Johannes Vilhelm Jensen, and Harry Martinson. Who today can name even one of their books? *Sic transit gloria.*

And yet for all our tardiness in recognizing literary worth, for all our lapses in literary judgment, we do know that an author and a book can make a difference. A great book—original in approach, significant and shrewd in its choice of subject—can, in Jefferson's phrase, be a "fire-bell in the night." The author of such a book can change the climate and culture of the time. Thomas Paine did so with *Common Sense*, summoning the American colonies to revolution. Rachel Carson did so with *Silent Spring*, directing attention to the urgent need for environmental protection. Betty Friedan did so with *The Feminine Mystique*, rallying the nascent energies of the women's movement. And Michael Harrington did so with *The Other America*, impressing on the nation the shameful living conditions of its poor.

Other writers have influenced the culture and climate of our time by distilling into a book an entire historical or social development, fixing it definitively in prose for succeeding generations of readers. Oliver Wendell Holmes, Jr., captured the moral spirit of our legal heritage in *The Common Law*, which I believe remains the greatest book written by an American lawyer. Gunnar Myrdal contributed to the Supreme Court's decision in *Brown v. Board of Education* (1954) with his book *An American Dilemma*, still the most comprehensive analysis of racial segregation in the United States.

Theodore H. White recorded the changing nature of presidential elections in his series of books entitled *The Making of the President*. David Halberstam caught the elitist arrogance of those who directed the war in Vietnam in *The Best and the Brightest*. David Riesman changed profoundly the way in which we think about the American character with his book *The Lonely Crowd*. Robert Coles revealed the remarkable resilience of children of every social and economic background in his series of books entitled *Children of Crisis*.

Although these two categories of books—those that were "fire-bells in the night" and those that expertly defined historical or social developments—do not include works of fiction, it is assuredly the case that fiction, too, has helped to shape our society. Abraham Lincoln reputedly jested to Harriet Beecher Stowe, author of *Uncle Tom's Cabin*, "So you are the little woman who wrote the book that made this great war." And Mark Twain, invoking a more dubious source of historical causation, blamed the Civil War on "Sir Walter Scott disease," the South's romantic idealization of a genteel way of life that never was.

The very best writers are those who speak to us across history long after they are dead, as readers of Dostoyevsky or Conrad or Dickens or Faulkner will affirm. Biographers, too, invoke the imaginative power of language to explore the mysteries of the human heart, as readers of Arthur Wilson's *Diderot*, Richard Ellmann's *James Joyce*, Leon Edel's *Henry James*, or Walter Jackson Bate's *John Keats* will attest. John Milton got it right when he wrote in *Areopagitica* that a good book is "the precious lifeblood of a master spirit, embalmed and treasured up on purpose to a life beyond life."

For most authors, who will never know whether their books will have staying power for future generations, few experiences can be more rewarding than knowing that their books have connected with people here and now. When books do that, an author experiences a rapture of satisfaction that redeems all of the effort that went into the writing, all of the uncertainties that attended the publication.

Holden Caulfield, the narrator of J. D. Salinger's *The Catcher in the Rye*, describes his experience with the magical phenomenon of connectedness between reader and writer:

> I read a lot of classical books, like *The Return of the Native* and all, and I like them, and I read a lot of war books and mysteries and all, but they don't knock me out too much. What really knocks me out is a book that, when you're all done reading it, you wish the author that wrote it was a terrific friend of yours and you could call him up on the phone whenever you felt like it. That doesn't happen much, though.

For many of us, I expect—especially those who, like me, first read *The Catcher in the Rye* when they were Holden Caulfield's age—J. D. Salinger is himself one of those rare authors whom we wish we could call up on the phone whenever we felt like it.

As satisfying as the acclaim of receptive readers can be, there remains for an author still another powerful source of gratification. That source of gratification is membership in a community of makers whose efforts help to shape the meaning of culture and civilization. Libraries are a locus of that community of creativity.

Libraries collect in a single place learning and literature of all sorts. They offer the collection, in its variety and quality, for scholars and common readers to examine. By taking into themselves the ordinary and the fabulous, the real and the ideal, libraries create a wondrous whole that is greater than the sum of the parts. That is what Archibald MacLeish, the poet who was once the Librarian of Congress, meant when he wrote:

> For the existence of a library, the fact of its existence, is, in itself, an assertion—a proposition nailed like Luther's to the door of time. By standing where it does at the center of the university—which is to say at the center of our intellectual lives—with its books in a certain order on its shelves and its cards in a certain structure in their cases, the true library asserts that there is indeed a "mystery of things." Or, more precisely, it asserts that the reason why the "things" compose a mystery is that they seem to mean: that they fall, when gathered together, into a kind of relationship, a kind of wholeness, as though all these different and dissimilar reports, these bits and pieces of experience, manuscripts in bottles, messages from long before, from deep within, from miles beyond, belonged together and might, if understood together, spell out the meaning which the mystery implies.

Libraries, then, are not ivory towers of hushed voices and lowered lights, comfortable sanctuaries on the margin of the world's rough strife. Rather, they are essential harbors on the voyage toward understanding ourselves. The strongest proof of the virtue of books can be found perhaps in the somber fact that for them authors have suffered exile from their native land, as Aleksandr Solzhenitsyn did; endured imprisonment, as Václav Havel did; sustained humiliation and insult, as Boris Pasternak did; and risked death, as Salman Rushdie does.

We celebrate libraries because we honor the word. A library salutes learning and the acquisition of knowledge. A library preserves the lessons of responsibility, freedom, and virtue. A library offers clear and captivating windows on humanity and culture. For all of these reasons, a library, as Shakespeare's Prospero believed, is "dukedom large enough."

Presidential Prose

During the years since I gave up teaching law to become a university president, I have reflected more than once on the rhetorical dimensions of the academic enterprise I left and of the one that I have taken up.

It is a truism among law professors that the greatest judicial opinions hold sway through their persuasive force no less than through their doctrinal soundness. The legal tradition has developed, in part, through judicial opinions ignited with rhetorical fire.

Our greatest judges—from John Marshall to Oliver Wendell Holmes, Jr., and Louis Dembitz Brandeis—have always understood the beguiling allure of the piquant aphorism and what Justice Benjamin N. Cardozo, in his elegant essay on "Law and Literature," called "the mnemonic power of alliteration and antithesis" and "the terseness and tang of the proverb and the maxim."

What judge has written a more rhetorically powerful statement than Chief Justice Marshall's bold insistence, in *McCulloch v. Maryland* (1819), that "we must never forget that it is a Constitution we are expounding."

What scholar has written a more rhetorically conclusive sentence than Oliver Wendell Holmes's sweeping pronouncement, in *The Common Law*, that "the life of the law has not been logic: it has been experience."

What moralist has written a more rhetorically persuasive exhortation than Justice Brandeis's exhilarating assertion, in *New State Ice Company v. Liebmann* (1932), that "if we would guide by the light of reason, we must let our minds be bold."

A judge's use of language is not a matter of indifference. Lawyers know, by training and instinct, that rhetoric has consequences. But too often the rhetoric that university administrators use to state their views lacks the energy and spirit that gives persuasive authority to the rhetoric of judges and lawyers.

One of the most important ways in which a university community develops a sense of itself is from the public statements of its academic leaders. Presidential prose can help to shape a university's vision of itself and to reinforce its sense of educational purpose. Yet university presidents are forever forced to avoid the pungent phrase, to blue-pencil the luminous metaphor, to give up speaking in their own voices for fear of causing controversy or giving offense to one or another group whose goodwill is essential to achieving the university's larger goals.

Although university presidents may draft their own public statements, they dare not issue them until they have been approved by dozens of colleagues sensitive to the concerns of the university's various constituencies. During that process of editorial approval, any brightness of language that may have lit up the president's first draft is inevitably made dimmer. Any element of personal style that may have lent grace or lucidity to the first draft is inevitably rooted out.

Thus, a firm assertion that "a liberal education is essential to the intellectual development of students so that they may discover who they are" is likely to emerge corseted with qualifiers, so that it states, limply and defensively, that "liberal education, broadly conceived, as a preparation for life, meets the functional needs of students by providing them with an exposure to the treasures of the past, an opportunity for social and emotional development, and a preprofessional experience that serves their career aspirations at the same time that it maintains avenues of upward mobility in a democratic society." The process deforms thought when it ought to refine it, homogenizes prose when it ought to sharpen it.

Given the public pitfalls awaiting presidential prose that aspires to individuality of style, is it any wonder that the rhetoric of university presidents is so often clichéd, prolix, wishy-washy, and unconvincing?

The Stillness and the Courage

What is the value of a liberal education? That question brings to mind Benjamin Franklin's famous remark when he was asked, as the Constitutional Convention came to a close, what was the use of the new document. "What is the use," he responded, "of a newborn child?"

The value of a liberal education, like that of a newborn child, depends, of course, on how it is nurtured. Its value depends on how it is made to shape, refine, and deepen our sense of self and others. If we let liberal education make a difference in our lives, it will.

This lesson was reinforced for me when I learned that I had cancer. I suddenly came face-to-face—as so many others have as well—with fundamental questions of value and meaning. The shock of that medical diagnosis brought home to me the meaning of F. Scott Fitzgerald's observation that "in a real dark night of the soul it is always three o'clock in the morning."

In my lonely hours of introspection, I came to concede for the first time the certainty of my own mortality and to understand the vulnerability of my being. I came to appreciate more fully that the time allotted to each of us is limited and precious and that how we use it matters. I knew these things before, of course—intellectually, even emotionally—but never with all my being.

I have been struck by two realizations—first, that life is a learning process for which there is no wholly adequate preparation; second, that although liberal education is not perfect, it is the best preparation there is for life and its exigencies. With it we are better able to make sense of the events that either break over us, like a wave, or quietly envelop us before we know it, like a drifting fog.

During the difficult and dismaying days of chemotherapy, liberal education helped me in that most human of desires—the yearning to make order and sense out of my experience. I have come to understand, for example, that literary modes—romantic, tragic, comic, satiric—are not mere academic constructs to which plays or novels may conform. Rather, those narrative categories exist because, as the Greeks and others have

51

understood for millennia, life tends to play itself out in ways that seem romantic, tragic, comic, or satiric—or perhaps all four.

Does liberal education answer all our questions and solve all our problems? Of course not. But, then, it does not pretend to. Show me a fictional character who thinks he or she has everything figured out, and I will show you an author's rendition of a fool.

Hearing a physician say the dread word *cancer* has an uncanny capacity to concentrate the mind. That is what liberal education does, too. God willing, both this disease and my liberal education will, each in its own way, prove to me a blessing.

What, then, is the use of a liberal education? When the ground seems to shake and shift beneath us, liberal education provides perspective, enabling us to see life steadily and to see it whole. It has taken an illness to remind me, in my middle age, of that lesson. But that is just another way of saying that life, like liberal education, continues to speak to us—if we have the stillness and the courage to listen. That reminder is worth more than gold.

2. Content and Character in Liberal Education

The Teaching of Values in a Liberal Education

Higher education inevitably presents the most troubling and perplexing questions concerning the teaching of values. In approaching those questions, one cannot escape the aptness of Judge Learned Hand's definition of the spirit of liberty: "the spirit which is not too sure that it is right." He was fond of recalling Cromwell's statement, "I beseech ye in the bowels of Christ, think that ye may be mistaken."

In recent years, the performance of colleges in confronting questions of values has been called into public question. This development should hardly be surprising. From the time that Jefferson emphasized the indissoluble link between education and democracy, American society has placed its greatest hopes—and fixed its greatest anxieties—on educational institutions.

In recent decades, public concern about the values Americans share—or do not share—has increased. The common core of values that once seemed to unify our society and to insure trust among the generations has eroded. As those values have lost their moral claim on our conduct, as institutions such as the family, the neighborhood school, and the church have failed to maintain their unifying social capacities, and as the younger generations have challenged the ethical standards on which their parents and elders have built their lives, society has turned its apprehensive attention to higher education.

Colleges are criticized by some (often by those whom we call "liberals") for not sufficiently teaching the values of *social* responsibility, while they are criticized by others (often by those whom we call "conservatives") for not sufficiently teaching the values of *individual* responsibility. Both sets of criticism, from the Left and from the Right, argue that colleges have, in Yeats's phrase, "lost all conviction." Still others argue that colleges ought not to teach values at all—that the enterprise of higher education ought to be value-free. These divergent points of view suggest that those of us who care about higher education must state our case with renewed conviction, as well as with clarity.

In too many respects, the tone of much of the recent criticism of higher education seems to me a contemporary version of "paradise lost"—

a version of social commentary that has had great staying power among cultural and intellectual pessimists from Henry Adams to F. R. Leavis. Many of the current critics of higher education are reminiscent, in their lament for the shining glory of a bygone world, of Edwin Arlington Robinson's character Miniver Cheevy, "child of scorn," who "wept that he was ever born." Robinson wrote:

> Miniver sighed for what was not,
>   And dreamed, and rested from his labors;
> He dreamed of Thebes and Camelot,
>   And Priam's neighbors.

Two of the most prominent recent critics of higher education have been William J. Bennett and Allan Bloom. The former secretary of education's views on the cultural deficiencies of liberal education, set forth in many public forums, and Professor Bloom's 1987 book, *The Closing of the American Mind*, have found responsive chords in American society.

Although I disagree with much of what Bennett and Bloom believe, I readily state my admiration for their commitment to academic excellence and their conviction that education must, among other things, be about book learning, hard questions, and answers worthy of consideration. But I have substantial reservations about their apparent willingness to rest liberal education so exclusively on the study of so-called great books, even though the works that are typically involved in such selections have, indeed, an undeniable power—moral, intellectual, and emotional—to set both mind and soul afire.

My reservations derive from a misgiving that the compiling of lists of "great books" risks our defining the intellectual and moral universe as closed and finite. It risks suggesting that liberal education is like a church with an authoritatively declared canon. It is, of course, neither. Liberal education is a process of inquiry, not a fixed body of knowledge, and its goal is the achievement of those intellectual and moral capacities that will enable students to lead lives that are thoughtful, reflective, inquisitive, and satisfying.

The aspiration of liberal education is to help students appreciate that the work of life is to grapple with the ambiguity of the moral universe and to ask searching questions addressed at defining the dilemma of being human, especially those questions that will unsettle their most routinely held beliefs. The aspiration of liberal education is to help students develop the intellectual, emotional, and moral resources to cope effectively with those desperate moments of disillusion that inevitably will darken their lives and cloud the assumptions that form the foundations of their being.

At the same time that Mr. Bennett, Professor Bloom, and others criticize liberal education for failing to teach values sufficiently, others question why colleges should teach values at all. Why, they ask, cannot colleges be indifferent to the values that students may acquire during their undergraduate years? Why cannot colleges just educate students, without seeking to impose any particular set of values, whether institutional or personal, liberal or conservative, on their students?

The answer, in my judgment, is that any mode of instruction, in any classroom environment, cannot escape the teaching of values. The pursuit of a liberal education is inseparable from the acquisition of values; that is so today, even as it was long ago found to be true at Padua and Bologna. There is simply no such activity as value-free teaching.

Indeed, a decision to pursue value-free teaching would itself entail the teaching of a specific set of values. All of us who are professors bring values to the classroom—values that we have acquired in the home and as adolescents, values that we have formed through reading and experience, values that we have employed to impose meaning on our own lives. To pretend that we do not convey these values to our students, as we profess to them, is disingenuous.

Colleges do inevitably teach values, and they do so by example. Students learn values by observing how professors perform in and outside of the classroom—professors who are dispassionate in their search for truth, careful in their weighing of evidence, respectful in their toleration of disagreement, candid in their confession of error, and considerate and decent in their treatment of other human beings.

Indeed, professors may teach most effectively about such values as integrity and honesty precisely when they admit to their own doubts or ignorance. There is no more important event in the moral development of a student than that quiet, suspended moment when a professor responds to an unexpected question by saying, "I don't know."

As students watch faculty members take risks in engaging the most difficult issues in the intellectual and moral world, as they observe faculty members exercise critical judgment by scrupulously weighing the claims of competing arguments, and as they hear faculty members express their own uncertainty as to where the balance of proof in a particular argument lies, they participate in a moral process. As students become familiar with the tentativeness and carefulness of a faculty member's cast of mind and as they learn that a professor may sometimes be puzzled or unsure when confronted with existential questions at the heart of his or her professional life, again they participate in a moral process.

The morality of a professor's example is perhaps the most powerful force in the teaching of values. By the power of their example, professors engaged in liberal education convey the humane significance of such values as inquiry, integrity, empathy, self-discipline, and craftsmanship. These are values that inform the academic process.

During the years that I was a law student, the prevailing themes of legal philosophy stressed the importance of process. That vision of the law emphasized the role of democratically empowered institutions in the settlement of conflicting political and social values, as well as the disciplined neutrality of the courts in enforcing the positive law. The leading theorists of that emphasis were Felix Frankfurter and Alexander M. Bickel. Justice Frankfurter taught us, in his famous statement in *Malinski v. New York* (1945), that "the history of American freedom is, in no small measure, the history of procedure." Professor Bickel, in *The Least Dangerous Branch* and other books, described and defended what he called "the morality of consent."

In recent years, John Rawls and others have argued that the law must be concerned with more than just process, that it must strive toward the achievement of certain substantive values, especially an equality in the distribution of income, social status, and economic rights. This development has brought with it a renewed concern for asking, "What does justice require of a society?" rather than "By what processes of authoritative decision making should a society define its views of justice?"

In many respects, the intellectual arguments taking place within the realm of legal philosophy are similar to those taking place on college campuses. And that returns me to Learned Hand—whose work explored, with an uncommon subtlety, the tension between process and substantive values—and especially to the Oliver Wendell Holmes Lectures that he delivered at Harvard Law School in 1958. In those lectures, published as *The Bill of Rights*, Judge Hand described the integrity and honesty with which the Harvard Law School faculty of his student days examined evidence and arguments; the skepticism they brought to the examination of grand theories, even theories of their own making; the balance they achieved in outlining opposing views; and the determination they summoned to establish the truth, in the face of irreducible inconsistencies and unruly and persistent anomalies. They were, he said, "a band of devoted scholars; patient, considerate, courteous and kindly, whom nothing could daunt and nothing could bribe."

It was these qualities of mind and character—qualities that are moral in the most important sense of the word—that led Judge Hand to conclude that "from them I learned that it is as craftsmen that we get our satisfactions and our pay." His own character was a testament to the hard-earned attainment of those values. And it is this lifelong commitment to mastery and craftsmanship, to inquiry and skepticism, that is, in the end, perhaps the most important of the transformative values that a liberal education imparts.

The Promise of Equality

Why is it important for colleges to educate a diverse student body? The issue is an important one because whom colleges educate is of paramount importance to our nation's future.

In *Brown v. Board of Education* (1954), the Supreme Court held that racial segregation in the public schools is unconstitutional. The Court's unequivocal affirmation of the equal rights of all citizens was, as Richard Kluger writes in *Simple Justice*, "nothing short of a reconsecration of American ideals."

We have made decided progress since *Brown v. Board of Education* in providing equal opportunities for the participation of minorities in our society. But the challenge of fully redeeming America's promise of equality—the promise set forth in the Declaration of Independence, in the post–Civil War amendments to the United States Constitution, and in the inspiring words of Abraham Lincoln—still lies before us, and with it the challenge of fully appreciating the necessary role of education in fulfilling that promise.

That challenge becomes more pressing—as a matter of social justice and economic necessity—as the proportion of minorities in our population grows. By the year 2000, no fewer than one-third of all Americans will be members of racial or ethnic minorities. In as many as five states and in more than fifty major cities, members of so-called minority groups will, in fact, constitute a majority.

The 1990 census found that our country's population stood at just under 250 million people. The white population grew by 6 percent during the 1980s and now constitutes 80.3 percent of the population as a whole. But the most striking findings of that census are those describing how four of the nation's minority groups all grew significantly faster than the population of whites. More than 12 percent of the country's population is now African-American, an increase of 13.2 percent over a decade before. Persons of Hispanic origin, who can be of any race, are estimated to make up 9 percent of the population, an increase of 53 percent. Asian-Americans constitute almost 3 percent of the population, an increase of 107.8 percent over ten years. And Native Americans comprise nearly 1 percent of the population, an increase of 37.9 percent during the past decade. In short, the racial composition of our nation changed more rapidly between 1980 and 1990 than at any other time in this century.

The striking demographic changes of the 1980s will have significant consequences for the nation's public school systems and colleges. By the year 2000, one-third of all school-age children will be minorities. These developments will also have significant consequences for the nation's workforce. By the year 2000, members of minority groups will comprise approximately 20 percent of the national workforce; in many cities and states that percentage will be substantially higher. At the same time, unemployment rates for African-Americans and Hispanics are and will predictably continue to be more than double those for whites.

These two facts—that minority groups are growing at a much faster rate than the general population and that unemployment rates for minorities are considerably higher than for any other groups—make it clear that American society must be more effective in the future than it has been in the past in providing educational opportunity for minority citizens.

Unless this country learns to take fullest advantage of the talents of all its citizens, we will fail to meet our own aspirations, and we will pay a high price in the continuing political and economic competition with other nations, particularly those of Southeast Asia and of the European Union. The alternative to an America in which all its members share in the opportunities and security that an education brings is, as Disraeli wrote in his novel *Sybil*, two nations "as ignorant of each other's habits, thoughts and feelings as if they were inhabitants of different planets."

Since at least the time of *Brown v. Board of Education*, it has been clear that educational opportunity is the single most important element in achieving economic advancement and fulfilling one's personal promise. As the Supreme Court stated in *Brown*, education "is the very foundation of good citizenship. Today it is a principal instrument in awakening the child to cultural values, in preparing him for later professional training, and in helping him to adjust normally to his environment. In these days, it is doubtful that any child may reasonably be expected to succeed in life if he is denied the opportunity of an education." For the reasons outlined in Chief Justice Warren's unanimous opinion, American colleges and universities have committed themselves to seeking out the widest pool of talent from among the nation's youth in an effort to strengthen minority representation in their student bodies and thereby to serve the ends of social justice and educational quality.

The nation's changing demographics mean that effective leadership in this country will require many more national leaders from minority groups—leaders in politics and public policy, in academia and the sciences, in culture and the arts, and in business and the professions. America's system of higher education has as its purpose today—as it always has—the preparation of students for positions of national leadership. If it fails to prepare young men and women who are minorities for positions of leadership, our society fails in an obligation essential to its renewal. This obligation is best described as a commitment to diversity. It is clear that there is substantial educational advantage to all our students, as well as to our faculty, from exposure to the knowledge, the experiences, the talents, and the perspectives of men and women of different races, nationalities, religions, and economic circumstances.

To the discussion of national problems, to the reading of literature, and to the understanding of history, students from minority communities bring perspectives that are very different from those of other students. It is persons least like ourselves who often teach us most about ourselves. They challenge us to examine what we have uncritically assumed to be true and raise our eyes to wider horizons. That was what Ralph Waldo Emerson meant when he wrote in his journal, "I pay the schoolmaster, but 'tis the schoolboys that educate my son."

A commitment to diversity—to educating able students from all quarters of our society—means much more, however, than a commitment to racial diversity. It means a commitment to geographical, intellectual, and economic diversity. It means seeking students from a broad range of communities—from Kodiak, Alaska, to Staten Island, New York; from Errol, New Hampshire, to East Los Angeles, California. It means creating a pluralism of persons and points of view. It means encouraging unconventional approaches and unfashionable stances toward enduring and intractable questions.

It means opening up our students' minds and our community's spirit to a symphony of different persons, different cultures, different traditions, and different languages. It means, preeminently, pursuing differences and otherness in all of their varied dimensions.

Most colleges have sought to create a diverse student body—with poets, athletes, and trombone players; actors, debaters, and butterfly collectors; young men and women of talent, ambition, and idealism. They have long recognized that, educationally, it is unwise to assemble a student body made up entirely of people who are very much like each other. A commitment to diversity is a commitment to educational excellence.

Difference sometimes means conflict. But conflict can be a source of creativity and growth if it is acknowledged with candor and examined with care. When people who are very different from one another must live and work together, tolerance and civility are the only hopes for peace. How we deal with our differences as Americans, how we nurture our shared bonds, will in large part determine the future character of our colleges and our society.

A large part of higher education's commitment to assembling a diverse educational community—and certainly the most expensive part—is seeking to ensure access to every qualified student, regardless of his or her family's economic circumstances. Colleges have a moral obligation and civic responsibility to do all they can to make the benefits of higher education available to qualified students regardless of financial need. As the economic gulf between rich and poor has widened in the United States, this commitment has assumed greater importance. America simply cannot afford to limit the benefits of higher education only to those applicants who can afford to pay.

As the cost of a college education escalates, colleges increasingly run the risk of drawing their students from the two ends of the economic spectrum—from families in the lowest income brackets, for whom scholarship assistance is most readily available, and from families in the highest income brackets, for whom scholarship assistance is not necessary. The losers in such a scenario will be students from middle-income families— not poor enough to qualify for significant financial aid awards, not affluent enough to pay the entire bill themselves, and often not aware that grant assistance is available for families earning as much as fifty thousand to sixty thousand dollars a year. A recent study has found that middle-income families tend to overestimate the cost of a private college education by about three thousand dollars.

Even if colleges succeeded in dispelling these misconceptions, the pressure on scholarship funds is only too real. Minority students receive a greater percentage of the scholarship aid than they constitute in the student body. The reason is plain: racial minorities in this country are more likely to need financial aid. Meeting that need constitutes simple justice and good sense for an institution dedicated to equal educational opportunity.

I have heard it suggested that, in these days of constrained resources, colleges may not be able to afford the "luxury" of directing a significant portion of their resources to scholarships. I reject that suggestion. It is important to remember that at many private colleges tuition covers only a little more than half of the real cost of education. At public universities, tax dollars subsidize the education of needy and wealthy students alike. This means that, in effect, every student at these colleges—including those paying full tuition—receives a substantial scholarship or subsidy. The difference between tuition payments and the overall cost of the education that a student receives is, in every instance, made up from endowment income, gifts, state appropriations, and other sources. And, so, the issue is not whether colleges should continue to dedicate a significant portion of their resources to scholarships but rather how large a particular student's subsidy should be—how those substantial resources should be allocated.

I have also heard it suggested that a commitment to diversity means a commitment to quotas. This is emphatically not the case. No college with which I am familiar uses quotas in its admission process. Colleges do, however, aggressively seek out and admit outstanding students from a broad range of backgrounds. Recruitment efforts include targeted mailings to students, special publications, on-campus programs for prospective students and secondary school counselors, visits to urban high schools, and the personal participation of minority alumni.

Those of us in higher education who are committed to the education of minority students are often asked whether African-American and other minority students are admitted to the student body in preference to white students of allegedly greater ability. The question disregards the significant subtleties of assessing ability and promise—as if colleges and universities have ever regarded ability and promise as ascertainable by SAT scores alone; as if we should equate the grades and test scores of students from among the weakest school systems in the country with those of students from the strongest; as if motivation, intellectual curiosity, and a history of availing oneself of what opportunities one does have should count for naught; as if colleges and universities had never followed a practice of admitting many students (whether they be athletes, musicians, or children of alumni) because of the special qualities they bring to the class.

The question also ignores the incontestable fact that, as Lyndon B. Johnson said at Howard University in 1965, "ability is not just the product of birth. Ability is stretched or stunted by the family you live with, and the neighborhood you live in, by the school you go to and the poverty or richness of your surroundings. It is the product of a hundred unseen forces playing upon the infant, the child, and the man."

Moreover, the question avoids the fact that the preferential treatment that many colleges' admissions process gives to children of alumni effectively puts minorities at a competitive disadvantage, since at most colleges the vast majority of alumni with college-age children are white.

There are those who argue that colleges and universities ought not consider race at all in the admissions process—indeed, that it may be racist to do so. I vigorously reject that argument. Regrettably, racial prejudice and racial discrimination still disfigure American life. Sadly, racial status still limits opportunity in American society. It is therefore inappropriate, in my view, to describe as racist those very admissions practices that would take account of race for the precise purpose of redressing the historic consequences of racial discrimination.

Justice Harry A. Blackmun, in his opinion in *Regents of the University of California v. Bakke* (1978), spoke wisely when he commented:

> It would be impossible to arrange an affirmative-action program in a racially neutral way and have it successful. To ask that this be so is to demand the impossible. In order to get beyond racism, we must first take account of race. There is no other way. And in order to treat some persons equally, we must treat them differently.

It would be ironic, indeed, as Justice Blackmun further observed, to interpret the Equal Protection Clause of the Fourteenth Amendment, which was adopted immediately after the Civil War in order to achieve equality for emancipated Negroes, in a manner that would "perpetuate racial supremacy."

Educators are called on increasingly to explain the causes of racial tension on American campuses. Why, we are asked, cannot minority students and white students get along better with each other? Why do African-Americans and other minority students sometimes seek to remain by themselves, especially in the dining halls?

In thinking about these questions, we need to remind ourselves that minority students are not the only ones who in fact are apt to sit together, in separate groups, at the same dining tables. So do football players and engineering majors and graduates of the same preparatory schools. No one notices when these groups of students sit together—or if they do notice, no one seems to find such conduct unusual. But when minority students choose to sit together—doubtless for much the same reasons as many other students do—some people do notice and some people do react negatively. My point is simply that we should use a single standard in judging the complex motivations of friendship and the need for social support that animate student behavior.

Moreover, the questions I have cited assume, erroneously, that efforts to attract minority students have created these social dilemmas. In fact, relations of equality between persons of different races is a relatively new experience in the history of this country. Many of today's students come to college without ever having had sustained interaction with students of different races or different economic backgrounds. Many lack a level of social ease with minorities, which in turn inhibits the ready development of personal relationships. We would be naive to expect these relations, at this point, to be free from friction or tension.

Students attending colleges and universities today—white and black, majority and minority—are part of a transitional generation, the members of which are learning to relate one to another in ways not yet entirely familiar and comfortable, but they are doing so with an earnestness and good faith that in the end will create a far better climate for the achievement of true equality than this country has yet known.

A certain degree of tension on the issue of race relations may actually be a sign of good health for an institution. The challenge is an educational one: to foster learning among students of diverse backgrounds by encouraging discourse, tolerance, civility, and engagement. More than ever before, we all have to live and work with each other. College is the best of those places where we learn to do so. And for all of the occasional points of tension, the success stories still far outnumber the moments of friction.

This, then, is not a time to pull back in our efforts to redeem the promise of equality. Rather, it is a time to strive, more patiently and more steadfastly than ever, to learn how to establish a society based on the practice of equality. It is a time for idealism, not cynicism; for healing, not wounding; for understanding, not indifference. The efforts to achieve diversity that are currently being made on the nation's campuses are an essential part of that learning experience. We need to support them with a vigor and fidelity that reflects their importance to America's future.

The Organization of Knowledge

In an age of abundant questions and scant resources, no university any longer pretends to teach all knowledge. Few even claim to provide an overview of the major divisions of knowledge. But in order to function at all, a university must have some system for organizing knowledge.

Knowledge is of little use to anyone if it is amassed unsystematically and retrieved indiscriminately. The enormous and shifting masses of information that accumulate unceasingly are unintelligible unless they are winnowed, sorted, and continuously rearranged to accommodate new material.

As a university's faculty selects the subjects it emphasizes in teaching and research, it ineluctably imposes a de facto order on the eternally evolving universe of thought. As these individual and collective decisions are made daily and hourly, the permutations of their combined effects become more and more difficult to calculate. With each course they prepare, each reading list they compile, each departmental course requirement they approve, each examination committee they sit on, each candidate whose work they evaluate for appointment or tenure, faculty members are shaping the body of knowledge that will come down to those who follow.

With each edition of the university catalog they produce, each library book they order—or cannot order—each budget recommendation they make, and each subject they choose for their next research or creative project, faculty members are helping to determine what will be remembered, what will be ignored, and what will be forgotten in times to come.

Because academic governance is decentralized, it is not always possible to detect a comprehensive principle of organization. As the bold academic initiatives of one generation become the sterile orthodoxies of the next, only to be rediscovered as creative innovations by the generation that follows, faculties too often appear to have adopted the timeless principle of Mae West, who once said, "In deciding between two evils, I always pick the one I ain't tried yet."

To a large extent, this impression of disarray is an illusion. The academic community does organize knowledge according to workable principles, but they cannot be expressed in simple prescriptions. That is because the ever-changing body of collective knowledge, like a living being, cannot be cast into a fixed and final form. As some branches of knowledge begin to bud, others are bursting into full flower, and still others are withering away. Some new programs strike root in fissures opened by the breakdown of exhausted systems of knowledge. Others arise in response to unanswered questions. And still others develop not from any internal educational logic but from the serendipitous presence of visionary faculty members or the beneficence of enthusiastic donors.

And so, little by little, a pattern emerges. The university's course catalog becomes a way of defining the shape of knowledge itself, a vivid exemplar of what the faculty holds most valuable in the human experience, and perhaps the most influential of society's models of the universe of thought.

A university president sees an institution's struggle to organize knowledge from a uniquely comprehensive angle of vision. During the years in which I have served as a president of two very different institutions of higher education, I have developed a profound respect for the authority that faculty members hold as inheritors and custodians of the academic legacy that one generation bequeaths to the next. I have learned that, as academic institutions and disciplines evolve, unresolvable tensions must always attend the organization and reorganization of knowledge. I have sensed the precariousness of the equilibrium between order and transition that holds a university together. I have arrived at a more sober understanding of the difficulty, the complexity, and the serious consequences of the choices that faculties must make in striving to impose an organization on knowledge.

In particular, I have come to see with increasing clarity that if academic decisions are unduly influenced by bureaucratic convenience, intramural power struggles, politically correct impulses, societal pressure to produce economically or socially beneficial results, or short-term ambitions, then faculties fail to take full responsibility for the organization of knowledge. And a failure to meet that responsibility means that a faculty will surely fail to pass on to its students a legacy commensurate with the one it received from its mentors. For all of these reasons, faculty members must shoulder a more conscious responsibility for the organization of knowledge and confront the need for crafting an open-ended system that allows for continuous accommodation and reevaluation.

Faculty members are charged with managing a repository of knowledge so vast, so rapidly increasing in volume, and so unstable in form that there is a real risk of losing all semblance of control. The more information that is known, the less time there is for reflecting on what is truly worth knowing. Computerized databases offer total recall and instant retrieval of material that twenty years ago would have been considered too ephemeral to justify preservation. Lists of new books in print risk becoming obsolete well before they are published, while hundreds of thousands of books printed in the last century and a half deteriorate more rapidly than conservators can decide which fraction should be saved. Even the most comprehensive cataloging systems cannot generate new categories rapidly enough to accommodate many emerging fields.

All too frequently, members of the same academic department scarcely comprehend one another's articles, if they venture to read them at all. As disciplines proliferate or take new directions, advisors are hard pressed to inform students about opportunities beyond a narrow range of familiar courses. And so the universe of thought expands with an explosive velocity. Even the areas of knowledge most closely related to our own seem to rush away in all directions. Information that once appeared just out of reach hurtles to the remote edges of awareness and then is lost altogether.

Scholars today share the frustration of Eugene Gant, Thomas Wolfe's protagonist in *Of Time and the River*, who as a college student

> would prowl the stacks of the library at night, pulling books out of a thousand shelves and reading them like a madman. The thought of those vast stacks of books would drive him mad: the more he read, the less he seemed to know—the greater the number of the books he read, the greater the immense uncountable number of those which he could never read would seem to be. . . . He pictured himself as tearing the entrails from a book as from a fowl.

Driven by such a passion for knowledge, cast adrift in such an unsettling intellectual universe, who has not yearned for the stately simplicity of the medieval curriculum, with its seven liberal arts so serenely arrayed on the classical framework of trivium and quadrivium? Who has not envied the Olympian assurance with which Bacon claimed "all knowledge" as his province?

But those orderly arrangements of the past were not, of course, so secure as they appear in retrospect. When Bacon undertook what he called "a faithful perambulation of learning," he boldly challenged the limits of the established order. As he argued in *The Advancement of Learning*: "Why should a few received authors stand up like Hercules' columns, beyond which there should be no sailing or discovering?" It was inevitable that Bacon's own meticulously drawn map of the cosmos of ideas would become, in its turn, one of the pillars of Hercules for another generation, and it was just as inevitable that the boundaries his successors marked would eventually be passed by yet later intellectual adventurers.

From Aquinas and Bacon to Jefferson and Newman, no conception has been more firmly embedded in the way knowledge is organized than the emphasis given to the values of Western civilization. Liberal education is widely considered in this country to be the surest instrument that Western civilization has yet devised for preparing men and women to lead productive and satisfying lives. But to the extent that an unqualified emphasis on Western civilization blocks access to non-Western civilizations, it stands as a pillar of Hercules. To the extent that an uncritical idealization of Western civilization legitimates an assumption of European and American cultural superiority, it, too, represents a pillar of Hercules. That assumption is as damaging to students individually as it is menacing to the world they will be compelled to understand and to shape.

As a corrective to that conventional emphasis on Western civilization, one need only recall the twelfth-century European discovery of scientific and mathematical works written in Arabic. It was not political or geographical barriers that had kept Western scholars from this body of knowledge until the time of the Crusades. Rather, it was a psychological and cultural indifference to non-Western achievements. But without the development of algebra, to say nothing of the concept of the zero and the Arabic numerals themselves, modern Western advances in mathematics and sciences would be, quite literally, unthinkable. Within less than a hundred years after the project of translating Arabic texts began, European scholars were able to enjoy the fruit of thousands of years of Middle Eastern studies in medicine, biology, mathematics, physics, and astronomy. Newton was right in saying, "If I have seen farther, it is by standing on the shoulders of giants." And faculties must remind themselves and their students, as they seek to organize knowledge, that the sturdy feet of some of those giants were planted firmly in the East.

The term *Western civilization* also stands as a pillar of Hercules to the extent that it is viewed as a fixed and final construct for organizing even that portion of knowledge that comes from the Western tradition. Of course we must continue to pay homage to what the poet William Butler Yeats called "monuments of unageing intellect." Of course we must continue to exercise our legitimate guardianship of the undisputed masterworks of our culture. But we must also take care that our respect for these monuments and masterworks does not stifle the growth of new knowledge. An ethic of interpretation and reinterpretation, of evaluation and reevaluation, is the law of intellectual life. Openness alone preserves us against ideological morbidity.

The toll of adapting too slowly to new schools of thought is severe. We marvel today that the Clapham Committee, writing in Great Britain just after World War II, could advise against establishing the Social Science Research Council because it regarded the disciplines involved as prone to "a premature crystallization of spurious orthodoxies." We marvel even more at the tardiness of a distinguished American university's announcement in the early 1980s that it had just approved for inclusion in the introductory humanities course Jane Austen's *Pride and Prejudice*— the first book by a woman ever to be studied in that course. The price of such a glacial response to new ideas is paid in the currency of lost opportunities for entire generations of students.

The University of Iowa paid this price in a celebrated incident in the nineteenth century. The case involved Professor Gustavus Hinrichs, builder of one of the nation's first and best-equipped scientific laboratories in a university setting, originator of a theory leading to the periodic classification of elements, developer of the prototype of the national weather service, and academic entrepreneur extraordinaire.

In one brief moment in 1871, during the ceremony inaugurating the Reverend George J. Thacher as the fifth president of the university, Professor Hinrichs's star was abruptly eclipsed. In his inaugural address, President Thacher captivated the Old Guard by announcing, "The time is fast coming when the recent loud outcry against the required study of Latin and Greek in our colleges will seem too absurd and even ludicrous ever to have been sincere; for it is one of the surest means of elegant and finished culture."

The battle that President Thacher precipitated between classicists and scientists led to the dismissal of Professor Hinrichs in 1886 and set back the development of the sciences at the University of Iowa for the rest of the century. It became a metaphor for intellectual pigheadedness. I daresay that every university president since then—as he or she has stated an intellectual vision on formal academic occasions—has had the recurring nightmare that historians may one day regard him or her as the Reverend George J. Thacher of the time.

Organizing metaphors owe their attractiveness, even seductiveness, to our deep longing for certitude. To speak of "branches of knowledge" is to imply that multitudinous fields of specialization arise from a common root. To refer to "streams of thought" is to suggest that diverse ideas eventually flow along common channels into a great reservoir of knowledge. But even as we use such expressions, we understand full well that the intellectual solace we may derive from them is at best temporary, at worst benumbing.

Indeed, that is why most colleges have abandoned the conviction that all students should study a single set of "great books." That is why we so often hear the lament that an academic catalog presents students with a bewildering smorgasbord of electives. Colleges have opened their curricula because they recognize that, in a pluralistic and evolving universe of knowledge, a university would be shortsighted to teach only those principles by which knowledge is organized at any one time. They recognize that the task of intellectuals and educators is to develop the organizing powers of the next generation of scholars, rather than to present them with a preselected packet of information.

It is the business of teachers to nurture those whose ideas, in time, will displace their own. The professor who presents a wide range of intellectual challenges and opportunities in a broad and humane spirit both preserves and disturbs the organization of knowledge. An educational philosophy that supports a candid presentation of order and disorder, of stability and flux, has the spaciousness both to accommodate and to precipitate revolutions in thought.

As colleges press on with the endless task of organizing knowledge, they must continually renegotiate the conflicting claims of preservation and change. They must provide their students with a solid grounding in those great organizational designs that for centuries have fed the human hunger for meaning. They must awaken their students' responsiveness to the restless energy that undermines other organizational patterns. They must allow students to experience the tenuousness and tentativeness with which still other organizing systems take shape.

But most important of all, they must help students to develop their own principles for organizing knowledge. They must arouse in them the determination to set about that task resolutely, despite the disquieting recognition that any scheme of organization they adopt can never be more than provisional.

When students are compelled to deal with alternative ways of organizing knowledge, they will also be compelled to consider fundamental premises. They will be required to seek out those patterns of organization that have the greatest explanatory power for specific kinds of inquiry. They will learn to choose organizing systems appropriate for their own inquiries, rather than merely to accept those schemes presented to them as received wisdom.

More than that, colleges must prepare students for the discovery that we do not fully understand how to relate one fact to another, one theory to another, one vision to another. They must brace them to confront the truth in a comment that Isaac Bashevis Singer once made: "The whole world acts out a farce because everyone is ashamed to say, 'I do not know.'"

If the academy is truly to make progress in the organization of knowledge, it must teach students to admit that they do not know. When Bacon caught sight of the pillars of Hercules that loomed across his own horizon, he did not hesitate to admit his own ignorance of the forbidden territory that lay beyond. Bacon has left us with the aphorism that all knowledge begins in wonder. It was sheer wonder at the gulf of ignorance ahead that urged Bacon beyond the pillars of Hercules. It is that same spirit of wonder, born of the repressed secret of our deeper ignorance, that should inspire us and our students to venture beyond our own pillars of Hercules. If we take that risk, we must ask, again and again, "How shall we organize what we know?" and "How shall we inspire our students to organize their own explorations of the unknown?"

As scholars clarify their answers to these questions, they will find a passageway between the pillars of Hercules that now bound our intellectual world. And they will fulfill their mission as scholars and teachers in participating more fully in Bacon's great adventure of the advancement of learning.

Science and Liberal Learning

Colleges committed to liberal education have a special responsibility to think about the meaning of science for the citizens of a democratic society. The achievements of science and technology offer fruitful opportunities and daunting dilemmas for every nation on earth. But particularly they pose challenges for nations, like ours, that govern themselves by democratic processes. For in such nations, citizens must be well informed in order to exercise their civic responsibilities wisely, and that is why colleges, having dedicated themselves to the education of young men and women who possess the high promise of leadership, must insist that liberal education convey an understanding of the laws of nature and of the achievements of scientific inquiry.

It is now more than thirty-five years since C. P. Snow delivered his celebrated Rede Lecture, at Cambridge University, on "The Two Cultures and the Scientific Revolution." In that lecture, he argued that "the intellectual life of the whole of Western society is increasingly being split into two polar groups": literary intellectuals and scientists.

Lord Snow described the "gulf of mutual incomprehension" that existed between the two groups—a gulf comprised of "hostility and dislike, but most of all lack of understanding" and "a curious distorted image of each other." He lamented that awful gulf because, as he said so well: "This polarisation is sheer loss to us all. To us as people, and to our society. It is at the same time practical and intellectual and creative loss."

The polarization to which Lord Snow so trenchantly referred was of fundamental importance when he spoke of it in 1959. It is still of great significance today. When a society's literary intellectuals (by which Lord Snow meant those persons who have received a classical education) cannot converse with its scientific intellectuals, so that each may gain an appreciation of the other's competencies and premises, then, as he wrote, "no society is going to be able to think with wisdom."

In the generation since Lord Snow described these "two cultures," the scientific revolution has changed our world at least as pervasively, some would argue, as the Industrial Revolution did the world of the nineteenth century. The disciplines that today comprise science and technology have made the world considerably more exciting—and more dangerous. They influence the form and content of our culture so extensively that virtually every major decision we make—whether it be political, economic, social, or moral—must take account of their accomplishments.

The implications of that influence for a democratic society are profound. The hegemony of computers has revolutionized the ways in which we compile information and manage organizations. The capacity of physicians to arrange for the conception of life in a test tube has created moral dilemmas of the most disturbing complexity. The availability of sophisticated life-support systems has presented perplexing legal and religious questions concerning the definitions of life and death.

As the achievements of scientific research have become more wondrous—in exploring space and propelling men to the moon, in harnessing nuclear power, in perfecting the most exquisite forms of genetic engineering—our society has responded with pride, rather than with understanding; with awe, rather than with edification. Science still perplexes us. We often sound like John P. Marquand's protagonist George Apley, in *The Late George Apley*, who complained to a friend, "Dear John: I wish there weren't quite so many new ideas. Where do they come from? . . . I try to think what is in back of them and speculation often disturbs my sleep."

Most Americans in positions of leadership want "to think what is in back" of scientific achievements, but they do not comprehend the basic principles of science clearly enough to do so. They lack an understanding of the relationship of the natural sciences to the humanities and the social sciences; they lack an appreciation of the poetry and drama of scientific inquiry. They lack, therefore, the full measure of perspective that is necessary to "think with wisdom" about the social and political consequences of scientific achievement and technological development. This is acutely disturbing.

There are many reasons to emphasize the importance of the sciences in a liberal education. Some are narrowly utilitarian. Education in the sciences, for example, will sustain this nation's fruitful tradition of scientific discovery and technological innovation—a tradition that runs from Benjamin Franklin, Thomas Alva Edison, and George Washington Carver to Percy Bridgman, Jonas Salk, and Barbara McClintock. In addition, education in the sciences will enhance this nation's ability to manage the complexity of a modern economy and to exploit fully the developing opportunities for technological growth. But more important than either of these reasons is our need to nurture an educated citizenry—a community of citizens that has the capacity to comprehend the impact of science and technology on the content and the direction of our lives.

As remarkable as the achievements of science so often are, they are neither inherently good nor inherently evil. They have both immense creative promise and, in Blake's phrase, "dark Satanic" potentialities. They may tell us that certain results are possible or predictable, but they cannot tell us what is politically prudent or socially just or morally fair. For the responses to such concerns—humane responses that can discern the boundary between scientific facts and the political, social, and moral implications of those facts—we must look to citizens and leaders who have been liberally educated.

Knowledge itself, as Francis Bacon asserted nearly four hundred years ago, is power. Ignorance is powerlessness and vulnerability. In endeavoring to empower citizens with an understanding of science, liberal education must emphasize that science is one of the magnificent achievements of the human mind—an intellectual activity of the greatest rigor, subtlety, complexity, and beauty. At its heart is a process of observation, testing, and critical thinking. By putting questions to nature, by putting hunches and hypotheses to experimental proof, scientists seek to establish what is true. That is no ordinary task, calling as it does on imagination, as well as intelligence and learning.

Liberal education must especially awaken students to the imaginative nature of the scientist's vocation, so that they can appreciate that the conduct of science is comparable, in fundamental respects, to the writing of poetry or the painting of pictures or the chronicling of history. Just as a poet seeks to express an understanding of the world by imposing an order on words, just as a painter seeks to convey a vision of reality by imposing an order on light and color and form, just as an historian seeks to record and explain the past by imposing an order on developments and events, so a scientist seeks to explain the riddles of the natural world by invoking intellect and imagination to impose an order on the disparate facts and phenomena that he or she observes. It is one of the obligations of liberal education to teach the vivid ways in which science serves the powerful human aspiration for an ordered explanation of the universe.

Turn-of-the-century novels contain many portraits of steamboat seamen who live in fear that the ship's boiler will explode. They develop a pattern of superstitions to placate the thirsty demons within the machine and thereby explain what they cannot understand. Although we may patronize these superstitions, most of us stand in the same relationship to twentieth-century technology as those seamen stood in relationship to that characteristic example of nineteenth-century technology, the steam boiler. Our lives, like those of the seamen, are served by technological instruments, the operational principles of which we do not understand—from telephones to compact discs, from microcomputers to nuclear power plants.

There is still another important aspect of science: the aesthetic experience it provides—in the exhilaration of the chase, the satisfaction of plumbing the unknown, the framing of the decisive generalization. Far from being a dry or heartless exercise, science is a pulsating activity of intuition and imagination.

The diaries and autobiographies of great scientists make clear, again and again, that inspiration was a prominent, if mysterious, source of their creativity. Ideas flash into the minds of scientists as unaccountably as lyrical phrases form in the minds of poets. "The father of geology," as the novelist Samuel Butler wrote, "was he who, seeing fossil shells on a mountain, conceived the theory of the deluge."

Scientists themselves often have difficulty explaining how their minds worked at those unpredictable moments when they hit on their discoveries. But the influences of metaphor and culture are fascinating to consider. Newton spoke of the universe that he did so much to explicate as a riddle (Keynes called it "a cryptogram set by the Almighty") and decoded it as much by the leap of his curiosity and the magic of his imagination as by any formal powers of concentration. His model of a clockwork universe, in which nature moves by inexorable law, is of course itself a metaphor.

Charles Darwin, in reflecting on the tide of evidence he gathered in the Galápagos Islands, wrote, "I am like a gambler and love a wild experiment." And later, "I trust to a sort of instinct and God knows can seldom give any reason for my remarks." Yet, in the end, Darwin's theory of natural selection bore a striking cultural similarity to the dominant laissez-faire economic theories of his time.

In our own period, James Watson, in *The Double Helix*, has given a memorable account of the discovery of the structure of DNA—an account that illustrates the way in which youthful arrogance, aggressive miscalculations, intense competitiveness, and imaginative (even impulsive) insights served to create perhaps the greatest intellectual revolution of the past half-century. Watson's aim, as he writes, was to show that "science seldom proceeds in the straightforward logical manner imagined by outsiders. Instead, its steps forward (and sometimes backward) are often very human events in which personalities and cultural traditions play major roles."

Liberal learning still confronts the challenge of bridging the "gulf of mutual incomprehension" between the two cultures that C. P. Snow warned against in 1959. It is a challenge to educate students of the humanities and social sciences to understand the natural sciences and their processes, to appreciate the resourcefulness of the scientific imagination, and to think wisely about the social uses and moral limits of scientific and technological achievements. It is a challenge, in short, to educate young men and women to be worthy of the responsibilities of modern democratic citizenship.

Liberal Education and the Legal Profession

As a law professor and law school dean turned university president, I have come to believe that there is, or should be, a tight and sinewy bond between the academic enterprise I have taken on and the one that I have left behind, for liberal education and legal education grow out of the same tradition of humane learning. Indeed, legal education can be no stronger than the base of liberal education on which it rests. And so I would like to consider the responsibilities that the legal profession has for improving the quality of liberal education.

Now, more than 150 years after the publication of the first volume of *Democracy in America*, de Tocqueville's observations are as fresh as ever. In speaking of the legal profession, he wrote, "If I were asked where I place the American aristocracy, I should reply, without hesitation, that it is not among the rich, who are united by no common tie, but that it occupies the judicial bench and the bar." From the earliest days of the Republic, lawyers have played an influential role in the determination of public policy. As members of the American aristocracy to which de Tocqueville refers, lawyers have joined their professional skill with their sense of social responsibility to provide policymaking leadership at the national, state, and community levels.

The conviction that lawyers have a responsibility to be policymakers was perhaps put with greatest force by Harold Lasswell and Myers McDougal in their important essay, "Legal Education and Public Policy: Professional Training in the Public Interest," arguing that "the proper function of our law schools is . . . to contribute to the training of policymakers for the ever more complete achievement of the democratic values that constitute the professed ends of American polity." This conviction has been reinforced by the widespread assumption that a legal education, by inculcating that mysterious art called "thinking like a lawyer," prepared persons trained primarily as generalists to take on policymaking responsibilities in the most substantively demanding areas of public concern.

Thus, lawyers have regularly ventured beyond their technical preparation in the making of public policy. The breathtaking legislative initiatives of the New Deal, for example, were conceived and administered primarily by lawyers. Similarly, lawyers have held dominant policymaking positions in many of the significant public initiatives in the decades since the New Deal—for example, the founding of the United Nations, the administration of the Marshall Plan, the creation of the Peace Corps, the waging of the War on Poverty, and the mounting of the civil rights movement.

In the making of foreign policy, too, lawyers have played a central role. More lawyers have served as secretary of state during the twentieth century than have members of any other profession. Because most of these lawyers had achieved professional eminence at the Establishment bar, it was doubtless assumed that they could readily master the complexities and subtleties of foreign policy.

And even when lawyers do not have direct responsibility for the making of public policy, they often exert a substantial influence on those who do. For this reason, it is important that the legal profession step forward to help the nation address one of the most prominent and important issues on the public agenda today: the issue of educational quality.

During the past decade, book after book, report after report, by educator or task force or blue-ribbon panel, has addressed the question of excellence—and the lack of it—across the broad spectrum of American education. The first wave of books and reports emphasized the weaknesses of the nation's high schools. Now we are in the midst of a second wave, and this one emphasizes the weaknesses of the nation's colleges and universities.

These books and reports—with the repetitive and persistent drumbeat of their warnings and lamentations—have captured the attention of the public, of the press, and of parents. They have provided new catchwords that, virtually overnight, have become a new generation of clichés. They declare—in the language of their titles—that the United States is "a nation at risk," obligated "to reclaim a legacy," compelled to make a greater commitment to "action for excellence," required to renew its "involvement in learning."

One of the first and the most widely disseminated reports, *A Nation at Risk*, published in 1984, gave us the memorable and menacing image of a "rising tide of mediocrity." And the most publicized report of the 1980s, *To Reclaim a Legacy*, charges that the humanities curricula in many colleges and universities have "become a self-service cafeteria through which students pass without being nourished," so that they remain ignorant of "a common culture rooted in civilization's lasting vision, its highest shared ideals and aspirations, and its heritage."

The shrill rhetoric of crisis that these reports employ, complete with apocalyptic predictions and flamboyant imagery, may cause some to overlook the disturbing substance of their conclusions. But the issues the reports raise and the problems they identify should not be ignored. If the legal profession is to continue to provide national leadership in the forging of public policy, it must once again be prepared to move into unfamiliar territory. Lawyers must once again apply their generalist training to help solve the specialized problems associated with strengthening the quality of higher education.

I want to suggest, first, why the legal profession has such a significant stake in the quality of higher education, and particularly the quality of liberal education. Then I want to enunciate two themes that I hope the legal profession will espouse in order to improve the quality of liberal education. And, finally, I want to outline the special contributions that the legal profession can make in the shaping of educational policy.

Lawyers should take a particular interest in improving the quality of liberal education, both for the sake of our society and for the sake of our profession. Education has been indispensable to the creation and preservation of America's democratic institutions. As the Northwest Ordinance of 1878 proclaimed, "Religion, morality, and knowledge, being necessary to good government and the happiness of mankind, schools and the means of education shall forever be encouraged." Between the beginning of the American Revolution and the end of the Civil War, as Daniel Boorstin has pointed out, a "college-founding mania" took hold of the nation. New colleges and universities sprang up rapidly and everywhere, and today the nation has more than three thousand institutions of higher learning.

The phenomenon of American higher education has intrigued and mystified foreign observers because, unlike educational systems elsewhere, it has no hierarchical structure or central organizing plan. It is hardly a "system" at all. Rather, it is a vast galaxy of institutions—large and small, public and private, nonsectarian and religious—uneven in quality, scattered with careless abandon across the reach of a continent. However puzzling it may be to foreign observers, our very lack of system proved to be a significant advantage in the shaping of a new society. Invigorated by an unconstrained spirit of adventure and experimentation, American education and American democracy have flourished and matured together.

As Allan Nevins wrote in his stirring history, *The State Universities and Democracy*, "The struggle for liberty . . . is always a struggle for equality, and education is the most potent weapon in this contest." The potency of that weapon for social change was well understood by Lyman Beecher, the Presbyterian clergyman, in 1836:

> Colleges . . . break up and diffuse among the people that monopoly of
> knowledge and mental power which despotic governments accumu-
> late for purposes of arbitrary rule, and bring to the children of the
> humblest families . . . a full and fair opportunity . . . , giving thus to
> the nations the select talents and powers of her entire population.

Beecher was talking about nothing less than the diffusion and redistribu-
tion of intellectual capital.

Nowhere is the intimate and reciprocal relationship between education and democracy more forcefully expressed than in the great educational and social experiment of the Morrill Act of 1862, an experiment that
not only established the land-grant institutions but also opened up a
calcified classical curriculum to the scientific and technological knowledge
of a new age and made higher education available to what the act called
the "industrial classes."

Rather than perpetuating an elite of gentlemen-scholars, the Morrill
Act called into being a wholly new kind of university, created without
European precedents, hospitable to all comers, and designed to prepare
Americans to be American. The land-grant university opened the pursuit
of excellence to the children of farmers, artisans, and storekeepers. The
founders of the land-grant institutes west of the Mississippi did not wait
for a network of preparatory schools to develop. They did not deplore the
miserable state of education on the frontier. They did not shrink from a
task that seemed impossible.

Instead, in the bold way of Americans, they grasped the importance
of setting high goals first and allowing practical solutions to develop in
consequence. And so they announced the opening of their classes and
offered remedial preparation to the adventurous handful of underedu-
cated students who enrolled; within ten or twenty years secondary schools
dotted the landscape. It was the creation of the universities that called the
community high schools into being. No wonder Emerson noted in his
journal in 1867 that "the treatises that are written on university reform
may be acute or not, but their chief value to the observer is the showing
that a cleavage is occurring in the hitherto firm granite of the past, and a
new era is nearly arrived."

Thus our aspiration toward the achievement of both goals—broad
accessibility and educational excellence—has been essential to maintaining and enlarging democratic values. As the educated classes have
expanded to include more women, more members of minority groups, and
more members of economically disadvantaged groups, our society has
reaped rich rewards. The broader the social base of those attending college, the stronger the intellectual base of our democratic society.

There is a lesson in all this for the legal profession: just as the developing land-grant institutions influenced the development of high schools and raised the general educational level of communities throughout the country, so the law schools can be a force for excellence in liberal education in the universities to which they belong. In exerting that force, the legal profession must take note of the fact that legal education and liberal education share common roots.

From before the American Revolution until the settlement of the West, liberal education and legal education recognized no dividing line. Humanistic legal studies at the undergraduate level were considered necessary to the proper education of eighteenth-century gentlemen and statesmen. Throughout the Age of Enlightenment, the formal study of law, then in its infancy, held a secure place in the liberal arts curriculum on both sides of the Atlantic. At Yale, for example, the Chancellor Kent Professorship of Law and Legal History was established in 1801, some forty years before there was a Yale Law School. Still earlier, when George Wythe and James Wilson presented their lectures on law to undergraduates at the College of William and Mary and the University of Pennsylvania, respectively, they were following a tradition set by Blackstone in his Oxford lectures of 1753.

In his book *Law and Letters in American Culture*, Robert A. Ferguson recovers the lost tradition of humanistic learning that provided a common context for legal and literary achievement in the first half-century of the new nation. Ferguson points out that lawyers made up half of the country's leading literary critics, wrote many of its major works of literature, and controlled most of its important literary societies and journals. As he notes, "no other vocational group, not even the ministry, matched their contribution" to the early American literary tradition.

Even country lawyers knew the Bible, Shakespeare, and Milton as thoroughly as they knew Blackstone, Mansfield, and the Constitution. John Adams, Thomas Jefferson, Alexander Hamilton, and James Madison were produced by the same literary and legal tradition that produced Washington Irving, William Cullen Bryant, Richard Henry Dana, Jr., and Francis Parkman.

Both strands of learning—the literary and the legal—concern themselves with the dilemma of the human condition, the consequences of individual decisions and actions, the tolerance of conflicting views, the balancing of justice and mercy, freedom and authority. These themes are the grist of the novelist's imagination, the poet's vision, and the essayist's insight no less than of the lawyer's craft.

The close traditional association between lawyers and literature has become increasingly difficult to maintain. But the law remains a learned profession, and it is incumbent on lawyers to champion and reaffirm the importance of the nexus between legal education and liberal education. The quality of the legal profession can rise no higher than the educational preparation of those who enter law school.

Students entering law school today were educated in a higher educational system that has gone through massive changes, including the abolition of many curricular requirements, a declining faith in the value of classical works of history and literature, and, most disturbing of all, a weakening of the self-disciplined will toward excellence. These students often have had no more than a dilettante's exposure to the central teachings of the liberal arts. Too many suffer from what Vartan Gregorian has called "historical amnesia." Too many know virtually nothing about the important universe of the biological and physical sciences. Too many have had scant experience with interdisciplinary inquiry. And too many have had only minimal acquaintance with international studies. These deficiencies would be a handicap for any citizen, but they are disastrous for students who aspire to the policymaking responsibilities that have traditionally been a province of lawyers.

And within law schools, no less than within undergraduate colleges, the insistent student demand is for specialized, narrow, practical preparation, not breadth of inquiry and general knowledge. Yet the world for which lawyers are being prepared will require, more than ever before, both more specialization *and* more breadth of knowledge.

The best lawyers will be those whose minds have been opened to the rich experience of Western and Eastern civilization; whose spirits have been enlarged by exposure to philosophy, art, music, literature, and drama; and whose horizons have been widened by the study of the natural and social sciences. A student who has been well prepared for law school will have gained experience in independent thinking, an appreciation of the interconnectedness of life on this planet, a capacity to challenge every form of dogma. A firm grounding in the liberal arts helps to elevate law students' aspirations, broaden their outlook, quicken their consciences, and heighten their sense of responsibility to their clients and to society. A lawyer who has not contemplated the enigma of the human condition will be a technician perhaps but a professional never.

Law schools have done their best to overcome the stigma of Burke's observation that the study of law sharpens the mind by narrowing it. They have sought to broaden their curricula by adding courses that draw on such disciplines as anthropology, economics, philosophy, psychiatry, and sociology. But efforts to broaden the law school curriculum have necessarily and properly been limited. The obligation of law schools to cover a widening expanse of basic ground constrains their capacity to make room for additional courses.

And so, if we are to broaden the preparation of lawyers for positions of public leadership, the most practical way to do so is to strengthen the liberal education they receive in their undergraduate years.

In acknowledging the significant stake it has in improving the quality of liberal education, the legal profession will, I hope, advocate the strengthening of two specific areas: interdisciplinary education and international education.

There have been many changes since the time when higher education comprised four basic disciplines: philosophy, theology, medicine, and law. But none is more striking than the way in which the university of the late twentieth century has become a tangle of specialties and subspecialties, disciplines and subdisciplines.

As our capacity to extend scientific inquiry has increased, as our ability to quantify historical and sociological analysis has become more sophisticated, as our ingenuity in criticizing literature and the arts has become more refined, the number of discrete areas of academic specialization has multiplied dramatically. At last count, American colleges and universities were offering 1,100 different undergraduate majors and programs. Of these, nearly half were in professional or occupational fields. One wonders, indeed, what an Aristotle or a Leonardo da Vinci or a John Henry Newman would make of the complexity of a modern university course catalog.

Too often, the increasing tendency toward specialization in modern universities has had fragmenting consequences for the life of the mind. As students of broad-ranging imagination find niches behind rigidly drawn disciplinary bounds, their intellectual horizons grow narrower. They learn to frame only those questions that can be addressed through the specialized methodologies of their particular disciplines. They become victims of what Ortega y Gassett described in *The Revolt of the Masses* as "the barbarism of specialization."

Without opportunity for creative discourse among educated persons throughout the university, without a broad understanding of the premises and assumptions of other disciplines, few dare pursue those expansive and untidy problems that push across the artificial barricades between disciplines. It is only by encouraging a collaborative dialogue among scholars and students in many disciplines that a university can fully explore the dilemmas that arise at those uncertain frontiers where the values of technology, medicine, and law confront the values of philosophy, religion, and ethics.

By insisting on the ultimate indivisibility of human knowledge, we will enlarge the range of our students' experience and encourage creativity in the discovery of new knowledge and the synthesis of new understanding.

And we will reaffirm our commitment to defining the university not chiefly as an ever-expanding, increasingly fragmented universe but as part of an integrated commonwealth of liberal learning—a commonwealth in which the contributions of every discipline are essential to achieving intellectual wholeness.

Not only should the base of liberal education be broadened to include greater emphasis on interdisciplinary education, but universities should also give increased attention to international education. As American citizenship has increasingly come to mean world citizenship, it has become even more important for policymakers to have an understanding of other nations, other cultures, other literatures, other modes of thinking, and other languages.

Since the conclusion of World War II, the United States and the other nations of the world have become increasingly interdependent, through political and military relationships, through international trade and transnational business, through exchanges of technology, and through scientific and intellectual cooperation. This process has been accelerated by the fact that, during the same period, the non-Western nations of the world have assumed greater political prominence and asserted greater influence than at perhaps any prior time in history.

For these reasons, the fortunes of this country are now tied inextricably to conditions in the many nations of the world. If we are to live peaceably in this world, our universities must bring a global perspective to liberal education so that our students can appreciate Eastern civilizations as well as Western civilization and can comprehend the awful complexities and promising subtleties of the international environment.

One of the United States' most distressing deficiencies is our growing inability to communicate with the other nations of the world in their languages. The study of a nation's language often reveals the values of a foreign culture more tellingly than do a dozen treatises. It illustrates the intimate connection that exists between style and content, between cadence and substance, between idiom and national character. It makes clear that human beings are as much the creatures of their language as they are its makers. It is only in recent years that American business has come to appreciate fully how important strong foreign language skills are to capturing sizable shares of foreign markets around the world.

Thus, it is clear that our national interests, both economic and diplomatic, require that we develop a versatile competence in foreign languages. And yet we have made little progress in doing so. During her tenure as secretary of education, Shirley Hufstedler pointed out that "in the Soviet Union, there are almost 10 million students of English, but there are only 28,000 students of Russian in the United States."

Similar ratios, which can only be described as alarming, exist for

Japanese and Chinese, despite the fact that the world is at the threshold of what many believe will be "the Century of the Pacific." Admiral Bobby Ray Inman, former deputy director of the CIA, warned in congressional testimony in 1981 that our nation's ability to gather intelligence has been severely compromised by our deteriorating competency in foreign languages, thereby "presenting," as he said, "a major hazard to our national security."

When Professor Richard N. Gardner of Columbia Law School returned from his service as ambassador to Italy in 1981, he asked a disturbing question: "Would anyone consider a foreign ambassador in Washington to be qualified who could not read the *Washington Post* or the *New York Times*, could not understand what was being said on the evening news, could not talk on delicate matters without an interpreter?"

Indeed, at the time of the war in Vietnam, not a single American-born specialist on Vietnam, Cambodia, or Laos was teaching in an American university or working in the State Department. And at the time of the revolution in Iran, only six of the sixty foreign service officers assigned to the United States embassy in Teheran were even minimally proficient in Farsi, the language that Iranians speak.

Moreover, as the locus of world politics and international trade is shifting from countries that speak English, Spanish, and French to countries that speak Chinese, Japanese, Korean, and Arabic, the United States is failing to keep pace in the education of men and women who can read and speak these languages.

It would be easier for all of us, of course, to continue insisting that the rest of the world learn English. But such an expectation has already placed Americans at a serious disadvantage in the international marketplace and at an even more serious disadvantage in diplomatic affairs. By expecting others to learn our language while we do not attempt to learn theirs, we are isolating ourselves from a wide range of opportunities—diplomatic, economic, and cultural. We are limiting our capacity to trade in ideas and understanding no less than in services and products.

The goal of international education must be to help our students to understand the values that other nations hold and the customs that they follow. The development of this understanding is not only important for enhancing our ability to function effectively abroad, both politically and economically. It is also important for reducing the costly and often dangerous misconceptions that so frequently result from cultural differences and for creating a foundation of international trust.

The challenges that the legal profession will face in improving educational quality, unlike many of those that have yielded to the mastery of lawyers throughout our history, cannot be met by such familiar lawyerly expedi-

ents as the filing of a lawsuit or the drafting of legislation that accommo-
dates competing interests.

One of the most disheartening aspects of American history is the
uneven, episodic nature of the attention that has been given to improving
the quality of education. When a deficiency is dramatically displayed,
Americans can be aroused to respond promptly, as they did in enacting the
GI Bill of Rights and in responding to the Soviet Union's launching of
Sputnik. But once the initial burst of response has subsided, Americans
have found it difficult to summon the patience to stay the course. And it is
precisely the capacity to stay the course that will be needed as Americans
respond to the many recent reports cataloging a decline in educational
quality.

Lawyers, more than other professionals, understand that a broad
measure of social consensus is an essential element of social cohesion,
especially in a heterogeneous nation of such diverse peoples and interests.
They understand, too, that only the formation of a social consensus—
drawing order, gradually, out of a welter of divergent views—can produce
lasting social change. That is why the persuasive arts of the advocate are so
urgently needed.

Lawyers appreciate as well that there are limits to the capacity of
specific institutions to produce social change. In no institution are these
limits more evident than in education. As Diane Ravitch has written in
The Troubled Crusade, "Probably no other idea has seemed more typically
American than the belief that schooling could cure society's ills." And she
concludes, "Sometimes schools have been expected to take on responsibility for which they were entirely unsuited. When they have failed, it was
usually because their leaders and their public alike had forgotten their real
limitations as well as their real strength."

The legal profession has a special capacity to point out that Americans have been slow to develop a sense of institutional competence and
institutional limits, especially in the making of educational policy. Too
often Americans have viewed education as a ready vehicle for the correc-
tion of deep-seated social ills of the kind that formerly were regarded as
within the domain of other institutions, such as the family and the church.

The present moment provides lawyers with extraordinary opportunities to exert policymaking leadership in achieving excellence in higher education. In exerting that leadership, lawyers must assert a vision of what an
emphasis on liberal education will contribute to American society. And
they must work with other leaders of the American community over the
long period of years that will be required to achieve these goals.

A liberal education that is enlarged to emphasize interdisciplinary education and international education will better educate our citizenry for the twenty-first century. And it will better prepare a new generation of lawyers to assume the responsibilities of leadership that will be required to sustain democratic values and social order in the next century.

The Lessons of the Law

As the speaker at a law school commencement several years ago, I told the graduating students that exactly thirty years earlier I had stood in a similar place as they did then and for a similar purpose, and that I believed then, as I had believed on that earlier day, that Justice Holmes was majestically right in stating that a person can "live greatly in the law."

Because the experience of a legal education is so intense and its subject matter so technical and complicated, it is easy to become consumed by details and to forget that lawyers have been educated that they may serve the public interest, and not only by litigating or drafting documents or representing clients on a pro bono basis. They also serve the public interest by helping ordinary citizens to understand and better appreciate the role that law plays in a democratic society.

All of us working in law would like to believe that we could offer to ordinary citizens a better account of our profession than does the judge in W. H. Auden's poem, "Law Like Love":

> Law, says the judge as he looks down his nose,
> Speaking clearly and most severely,
> Law is as I've told you before,
> Law is as you know I suppose,
> Law is but let me explain it once more,
> Law is The Law.

We would like to believe that, unlike Auden's judge, we would have the capacity to explain to ordinary citizens that the law is a set of reasonable rules for governing society, a matrix of requirements, practices, and understandings that promotes public order, regulates personal and business relationships, and provides guidelines of fairness and common sense. Yet, for all of our explanatory competence, we know that most Americans perceive the law quite differently—as a bramble bush of alienation and a thicket of mystification ("a sort of hocus-pocus science," as Charles Macklin, an eighteenth-century playwright, once said). The persistence of these perceptions of alienation and mystification means that lawyers devoted to

93

public service have their work cut out for them. For who are better than lawyers for describing to ordinary citizens the great lessons that the law has to teach?

Most Americans would be surprised by the concept of the law as teacher. They typically think of the law as prohibitor, as adjudicator, as arbitrator—as anything but teacher. This is cause for lament, for the law has much to teach. In my commencement speech, I chose to focus on three lessons I have learned in thirty years at the bar. They are lessons that concern the responsibilities of citizenship, the limitations of expertise, and the complexity of context.

Democracy is the most demanding of all political arrangements. It asks ordinary men and women to meet the extraordinary responsibilities of citizenship. One of the most important ingredients in meeting those responsibilities is an understanding that although the law seeks to rest its aspirations on reason, the "life of the law," as Justice Holmes taught us, "has not been logic: it has been experience." As all lawyers have learned time and again, the law is not an inert body of static principles but a vital organism that is constantly evolving in response to social change.

Citizens who do not understand this fact will hold the law to inappropriate and unrealistic expectations. They will expect of the law an abstract perfection that cannot be attained, and as a result they are apt to be discouraged from participating in the democratic process.

Justice Holmes also taught us that the theory of our Constitution is "an experiment, as all life is an experiment." The mysterious process by which free men and women govern themselves by law is indeed an experiment, a perilous one that is hardly assured of continuing success. That process requires us to question the values and institutions we have inherited from the past, even as we seek workable and principled answers by which to live for the present. It requires us to recognize that the provisional working answers that every generation formulates in order to govern itself will inevitably pose new and differently phrased questions for the generations yet to come.

This country's experiment in democratic government depends on the qualities that ordinary citizens bring to that process of intergenerational dialogue: self-discipline, patience, historical perspective, and a tolerance for ambiguity. Through education and by instinct, lawyers know much of this lesson. They need to help ordinary citizens to know it, too, because the future of the democratic experiment depends on the continuing cultivation of such broad-based understanding and the ongoing exercise of the responsibilities of citizenship.

The law's second lesson concerns the limitations of expertise. When ordinary citizens become impatient with the compromises and untidiness required by the process of making and administering the law, they often crave the ostensible comforts and security of expertise. How easy it is to ask experts to make those judgments that seem beyond the powers of ordinary citizens! But resorting to expertise is no substitute in a democracy for the informed expression of the people's political will. As the problems facing our society become increasingly technical, one of the most effective ways in which lawyers can serve the public interest is by helping ordinary citizens to appreciate the limitations of expertise.

In looking back more than a half-century to those who framed the ideology of the New Deal, one is struck by their faith in expertise as a principal attribute of administrative regulation. Thus, James M. Landis, in a classic essay written in 1938, argued that with

> the rise of regulation, the need for expertness became dominant; for the art of regulating an industry requires knowledge of the details of its operation, [the] ability to shift requirements as the condition of the industry may dictate, the pursuit of energetic measures upon the appearance of an emergency, and the power through enforcement to realize conclusions as to policy.

Felix Frankfurter, like Landis, believed that if public regulation were to be effective as an instrument of social and economic reform, Americans would have to rely, as the British had done, on "a highly trained and disinterested permanent service," one that is charged not only with administering governmental policies but also with "putting at the disposal of government that ascertainable body of knowledge on which the choice of policies must be based."

The faith that Landis and Frankfurter had in the utility of expertise was based on an idealized conception of government. Few persons of the intellectual stature of Landis and Frankfurter would today celebrate the possibilities of administrative expertise with a similar enthusiasm. Expertise is too often narrower than the full reach of the social problem it seeks to solve or is too specialized to reflect the best interests of society as a whole. Moreover, it is seldom—if ever—entirely disinterested or devoid of political considerations.

We must be careful, of course, to preserve opportunities for the law to take measured advantage of what specialists can usefully offer as demographers, economists, engineers, psychologists, scientists, and statisticians. But the experience of the last sixty years has shown that the undoubted contributions of expertise must be placed in a larger context of relevant considerations and can be no more than one variable in the complicated calculus of democratic decision making. By helping ordinary citizens to appreciate the limitations of expertise in the making of public policy, lawyers can play a significant educational role.

Finally, lawyers can serve the public interest by enabling ordinary citizens to understand the importance of considering legal and social change within the complexity of context. This third lesson is a necessary antidote to the unrealistically ambitious expectations that many people hold about what society can accomplish through the sheer force of legislation or litigation alone.

The law does not exist in a vacuum. The fate of virtually every major political movement in American history—whether it be to abolish slavery, to establish suffrage for women, or to affirm equal opportunity for all citizens—has turned not only on the law but also on the social context in which it occurred. Other examples abound. The drive to secure the rights of workers to organize and to bargain collectively originated in a political and social movement, but it could not have achieved its goals without the legitimating support of the law. By endorsing the creation of both a framework of employee rights (the Wagner Act) and a forum in which those rights could be vindicated (the National Labor Relations Board), the law served as society's teacher.

Similarly, the law reinforced and validated the political and social goals of the civil rights movement by expressing, in the landmark judicial decisions and legislation of the 1950s and 1960s, the values of equality—particularly in *Brown v. Board of Education* (1954), the Civil Rights Act of 1964, and the Voting Rights Act of 1965. Without the symbolic validation and public authority that the law placed behind the civil rights movement, that movement's goals could not have been realized.

In both of these areas, as in so many others, it would be difficult for historians to determine precisely the reciprocal extent to which the law followed the social movement and the social movement followed the law. But it is certain that without the moral, social, and political pressure of the labor movement and the civil rights movement, the law would not have been changed. And had the law not been changed, the moral, social, and political force of both of these movements would have been diluted and perhaps frustrated.

When lawyers educate about the law's role in consolidating and legitimating social change, they are teaching about the pressures of context. It was Edmund Burke who wrote, "Circumstances (which with some gentlemen pass for nothing) give in reality to every political principle its distinguishing colour, and discriminating effect. The circumstances are what render every civil and political scheme beneficial or noxious to mankind."

It is important for Americans to understand, therefore, that in every major wave of historical change, the impact of political, social, and legal influences on the outcome is invariably mutual and reciprocal. Context matters. A new legislative act or judicial decision almost always represents an accommodation. It rarely gives any single contending force precisely what it wants, even if that force represents a decisive majority. In the pragmatic world of legislative and judicial decision making, the more sharp-edged wishes of the majority are almost always compromised (as James Madison counseled they must be) by the pressures and complexity of context.

For me, then, one of the essential ways in which lawyers can effectively serve the public interest is by educating ordinary citizens in the realistic uses and true nature of the law. Certainly those citizens will hear all around them other voices, making more frightening claims for the nature of law—as the poet Auden, again, understood so well:

> Others say, Law is our Fate;
> Others say, Law is our State;
> Others say, others say
> Law is no more
> Law has gone away.
>
> And always the loud angry crowd
> Very angry and very loud
> Law is We,
> And always the soft idiot softly Me.

This law of the "loud angry crowd"—the law of the mob and of the "soft idiot"—is finally the result of a dark descent into accepting simple, nihilistic responses to the complicated, nuanced challenges of participatory democracy.

As each new generation of law students enters the profession of lawyering, I hope that its members think of themselves not only as careful and caring practitioners of the law but also as educators of ordinary citizens, and that in their lives as lawyers, they demonstrate the lessons that the law teaches: the lessons of democratic responsibility, the limitations of expertise, and the complexity of context. For in these lessons lie keys to the achievement of the public interest.

The Professor's Life

Someone has defined a university president as a person who shuttles between God and Mammon. In the course of my own efforts to preach the hallowed ideals of the university while seeking the financial means of bringing them into reality, I am continually struck by the contrast between what those outside the university believe that professors do and what they do in fact.

Viewed from outside academe, the life of a university professor seems sheltered from everyday reality, a haven for those too delicate and sensitive to succeed in the workaday world. Few understand that the life of a professor is a difficult, lonely, and dedicated one. It is a life of privilege, to be sure—of autonomy in the classroom, of control over the use of time, of free inquiry, of tenure. But in return for those privileges, a professor pays exacting costs in ways that are rarely visible to people who are not academics.

The first of those costs is the continuous struggle to learn afresh what remains fundamental about a discipline that is always evolving, while bringing that knowledge to life in the minds of new students. One of the themes of Carl Sandburg's autobiography, *Always the Young Strangers*, is the renewal of society in every generation by the emergence of "young strangers"—young people who have the ability to lead their contemporaries to renew the values that sustain our culture. In the course of a semester, professors have only so many opportunities to reach those young strangers. A carelessly read term paper, a poorly conceived assignment, a flatly delivered lecture—any shortcoming in instruction—wastes an opportunity and violates their contract with those impressionable young strangers. That is why professors must work for so many hours in preparing courses they are teaching for the second, third, or even twentieth time.

A second cost is the struggle to compress a host of protean and unruly tasks into a day that is always too short. A professor's enormous flexibility in the use of time, so incomprehensible to people who are not academics, is undeniably a great privilege, but it is purchased at a price. In the absence of a clear boundary separating vocation from avocation, teaching from scholarship, creative effort from routine chores, no single block of time can be protected from a flood of conflicting but equally legitimate demands.

Consider the quandary created by three unscheduled hours between classes on a given afternoon. Should a conscientious professor spend those hours refining the next classroom presentation, checking on new library acquisitions, catching up with reading in professional journals, doing research for a new article, double-checking a dubious experimental result, drafting a committee report, conferring with students who need extra attention, writing letters of recommendation, preparing a budget for a grant application, or revising the syllabus for next semester's course? Indeed, those golden unscheduled hours, so apparently free in prospect, are in actuality already oversubscribed before the day begins.

A third cost—one that can never be paid in full—is the responsibility to create new knowledge, whether in the library, the laboratory, or the studio. If it is difficult for those outside academe to understand what a professor must do to teach well, it is even more difficult for them to understand what a professor must do to contribute to new knowledge.

Professors may not have faced the need to meet a payroll, in the vernacular of the marketplace, but they have experienced a severe trial of their own: they have lived intimately with agonizing doubt about the value of their labors. They are confronted by unceasing questions: Does this finding truly shed new light on a murky problem? Is this experiment as well designed as it should be? Has this idea been expressed with sufficient clarity? Will this undertaking ever produce a useful result? Will others appreciate its significance? Because the search for knowledge is open-ended, there can be no point of conscientious rest.

During the unending struggle to make sense of the unknown, the scholar's identity hangs always in the balance. When a professor confronts the emptiness of the unwritten page, the silence of the laboratory instrument, the blankness of the computer screen, all certainties evaporate. As W. H. Auden wrote of his own experience as a poet:

> In the eyes of others, a man is a poet if he has written one good poem. In his own, he is only a poet at the moment when he is making his last revision to a new poem. The moment before, he was still only a potential poet; the moment later, he is a man who has ceased to write poetry—perhaps forever.

So it is with the woman or man who is a scholar. The identity of the true scholar, no matter how much he or she has already achieved, is always at risk. The next book, the next poem, the next scientific finding, the next work of art may never come—or so it seems when the capricious muse of scholarship has departed, leaving only the gathering fear that it will never return.

A fourth cost of the professional life is the obligation to repay society's heavy investment in the protection of independent thought. This obligation rests on perhaps the least understood of all the privileges of a professor's life, the protection provided by tenure. Outside of academe, tenure is frequently misunderstood as conferring a sinecure. But tenure has nothing to do with job security in the ordinary sense. Its primary purpose is to serve society's need for independent criticism and a continuous flow of new ideas. The creation of knowledge is inherently threatening to the existing order. It disrupts the pieties of a settled past, the complacencies of a comfortable present, and the prognostications of an assumed future. That is why the search for knowledge is so closely controlled in so many other societies. And that is why, in a free society, tenure is so important.

Tenured scholars are free to choose topics for scholarship, without regard to political or economic pressure. They are free to persist in investigations that may require an extended period of gestation before they bear fruit. They are free to explore new and unconventional areas of inquiry without the pressure of having to reach conclusions prematurely. They are free even to bite the hand that feeds them, by criticizing the very institutions on which their intellectual and financial security depends. As Learned Hand said in paying tribute to his former law professors, "In the universe of truth, they lived by the sword; they asked no quarter of absolutes and they gave none." In the end, tenure serves the best interests of society by guaranteeing some of the most promising minds of every generation an unhurried opportunity, free from external constraints and the intellectual fashions of the moment, to investigate fundamental human concerns.

In return for the extraordinary privilege of tenure, much is expected. As mature scholars, professors have a clear obligation to fulfill the promise held out by their early achievements. They have a responsibility to press toward the frontiers of what is already understood, if only by a handful of specialists, in order to enlarge what the rest of us know. They have an obligation to raise hard questions, take unpopular positions, and accept intellectual risks—in short, to build up a significant body of excellent work that opens new horizons for their successors.

The effort required to meet all these obligations is prodigious. The life of a professor is not for the fainthearted. It demands uncommon fortitude. It is a high calling, aptly described by the intellectual historian Jaroslav

Pelikan as "a sacred vocation." It is a profession fit only for those who understand Emerson's succinct admonition in "The American Scholar": "There can be no scholar without the heroic mind."

But just as the costs of a life of scholarship and teaching are largely invisible outside the academic community, so are its unique rewards. The reward that animates every scholar is the joy of discovery—the satisfaction of finding out what no one else knows and of making that knowledge available to others. At the heart of that joy is the sublime delight of getting something absolutely, unmistakably *right*. That is the joy that laboratory scientists feel when they devise an experiment that not only works the first time but can also be flawlessly replicated and verified by others. That is the joy that mathematicians feel when they know that their colleagues will recognize their theorems and proofs as "elegant." That is the joy that essayists feel when they liberate an idea from the modish jargon of a single discipline and offer it to the larger community of students and scholars.

Surely a scholar's most substantial reward is what Oliver Wendell Holmes, Jr., called "the secret isolated joy of the thinker, who knows that, a hundred years after he is dead and forgotten, men who have never heard of him will be moving to the measure of his thought." Holmes called that satisfaction "the subtle rapture of a postponed power."

At the close of long days of work, at the conclusion of long years of scholarly solitude, professors are entitled to feel that rapture, to recognize that their teaching will create a ripple of influence that will be felt in the lives of students years after graduation. They need to be reassured that although their scholarship may appear in obscure journals and be read by perhaps only twenty or thirty of their colleagues today, it may set an agenda for research that will shape a discipline for years to come. They need to be reminded that future generations will indeed move to the measure of their thought. But professors, like all others whose identity is closely tied to their professional achievements, also need immediate and tangible gratification.

In a period of intensified competition for limited financial resources, professors, as well as college presidents, must understand that academic excellence is not only its own reward but also a key that unlocks the coffers of Mammon. And presidents, as well as professors, must understand that the measure of the scholar's thought is the source of a university's vitality and the standard by which it must judge itself. Nothing else, not even the most lavish favors granted by Mammon, has value except as a means to that end.

3. Models for Shaping a Life

Public Selves, Private Selves

In his great novel *Doctor Faustus*, Thomas Mann wrote: "There is at bottom only one problem in the world and this is its name. How does one break through? How does one get into the open? How does one burst the cocoon and become a butterfly?"

The college years are, of course, years of personal development, years when students prepare to "burst the cocoon" and "get into the open." They are years in which students confront the question of how to shape a life that is satisfying and meaningful. As each of us of an older generation can attest, such satisfaction and meaning do not come easily. But they are most likely to be earned by those who appreciate the importance of nurturing and integrating two separate selves: a "public self" that is committed to discharging the responsibilities of citizenship and a "private self" that is dedicated to developing the capacities to reflect, to create, and to understand.

Personal growth comes from many sources, but none is more important than a dedicated commitment to social and public responsibilities. Because we share a common society—indeed, a common world—with our fellow men and women, we share a common obligation to work to improve that society and that world. Not everyone can be a senator, governor, congressperson, or ambassador. Not everyone will stride across the national stage of public events. But everyone can make effective contributions to the quality of life in the communities in which we live. Every one of us can devote ourselves to strengthening the public institutions that enrich our communal life—by service on city councils and local school boards; by support of art museums and symphony orchestras, hospitals, and shelters for the homeless; and by grassroots participation in public debate and electoral campaigns.

And, so, I urge students to commit themselves, during their college years and beyond, to a public responsibility worthy of their talents and idealism. By doing so, they will not only help to make our society a better place in which to live, they will also "get into the open" and place themselves on a path toward self-definition. And I remind them, as they make that commitment, of Goethe's sobering warning that we must take care in

105

choosing our ambitions when we are young, because in later years we are likely to achieve them in abundance.

As students commit themselves to defining a public self, I hope that they will also commit themselves to defining a private self: a self that yearns to understand the vast mysteries of creation and the universe; a self that can find peace in the still, dark hours of the night; a self that can address grief and tragedy and the terrible misunderstandings that can arise among the generations; a self that responds to poetry and music and dance; a self that is renewed by reflections and contemplation.

I express the hope that students will find time throughout their lives for the cultivation of pursuits that add texture and mystery to life— whether it be reading philosophy or maintaining dear friendships or playing the piano or keeping a journal. I hope, in short, that they will cultivate the means of discovering themselves.

And I urge them to strive to balance and integrate these two separate parts of themselves—the public and the private—because too great an emphasis on the public self can lead to self-importance and self-centered ambition, while too great an emphasis on the private self can lead to self-indulgence and a selfish individualism. Striking and maintaining this balance is never easy, but if one succeeds in integrating these two selves into a coherent whole, he or she will have become a human being whose life will be satisfying and meaningful indeed.

Because such human beings are unusual, they exert an influence on others, well out of proportion to their numbers. Each of us has had exemplars in his or her own life—men and women who have been our heroes and who have set for us standards of what it means to be a whole human being.

Two such persons who have been sources of my own vision of what the Greeks call "exercising vital powers along lines of excellence" were my teacher at Yale Law School, Alexander M. Bickel, whose untimely death in 1974 is still an occasion for mourning, and my first employer, Thurgood Marshall, the leading civil-rights lawyer of his generation. Professor Bickel and Justice Marshall were very different individuals, but they exemplify the kind of balancing of public and private values that enables men and women, concerned with the shaping of satisfying and meaningful lives, to find their own particular way of bursting the cocoon and getting out into the open.

Alexander Bickel was a teacher and a scholar, a man of the book, an elegant intellectual who challenged and deepened our understanding of the function of law in a democratic society. Thurgood Marshall was a pragmatic lawyer and earthy tactician, a dynamic mobilizer of men and women, a man of action who devoted his extraordinary talents to the most important law-reform effort of the twentieth century. Professor Bickel advanced the law by the development of theory. Justice Marshall advanced the law by the perfection of practice. Each, in his own way, addressed the larger, humane questions that infuse law and life with significance.

The most important lesson that Alexander Bickel taught to me and to an entire generation, in the classroom and through his luminous writings, was the importance of process—what he called "the morality of consent"—and of the procedures by which public decisions are reached. From him I learned, as he had learned from Edmund Burke, that adherence to the time-tested processes of the legal order (however frustrating they may sometimes seem) is more important to the practice of statecraft than is the achievement of any momentary political result. He emphasized that the democratic institutions that England and the United States have developed during several hundred years of trial and error (however imperfect they remain) provide the stability that is essential for expressing, as well as constraining, the majority's will.

My second hero, Thurgood Marshall, is one of the only persons ever to sit on the Supreme Court who would deserve a leading place in American history even had he never been appointed to the nation's highest court. For it was Thurgood Marshall, prior to becoming a Supreme Court justice, who directed the legal effort that culminated in the Supreme Court's 1954 decision in *Brown v. Board of Education.*

Justice Marshall taught me the indispensability of legal craftsmanship and the moral obligation to put that craftsmanship in the service of a significant public cause. In his case, that cause was the achievement of an integrated society based on the central value of our legal and political system: equal justice for all citizens. Through his actions, as well as his words, Justice Marshall taught me that a citizen's finest opportunity is not to make money, and not to seek fame, but to ally both self and talent with an idea whose time has come. And Thurgood Marshall also taught me that a person can mount a determined assault on even the meanest and most provocative injustices without surrendering his humanity or descending into a bitterness toward his adversaries that, in Yeats' phrase, makes "a stone of the heart."

Alexander Bickel and Thurgood Marshall represent two different strands in American culture—the contemplative and the active—strands that I hope students will come to admire, in equal measure, as they burst the cocoon and get into the open. Both of these men dedicated themselves to the public lives of effective citizenship and to the achievement of a more just society. Both refined their private selves by wide reading and never-ending reflection on the nature of a democratic commonwealth and of a free people's institutions. By mastering their own discipline, both men transcended it. By transcending themselves in their work, they found themselves again, in the human community beyond.

Professor Bickel and Justice Marshall teach us, by their example, that the processes of managing a democratic society and of conducting a moral life are both dynamic ones. They are processes that require a continuing dialogue about which of our inherited values are bedrock and which are merely convenient and conventional; a dialogue between the generations that have come before and our own generation; a dialogue between our own generation and the generations that will come after; a dialogue between our public selves and our private selves.

I have great faith that as this generation of college students bursts the cocoon and gets out into the open, it will continue that process of dialogue. One of the themes of Carl Sandburg's autobiography, *Always the Young Strangers*, is the way in which every society, in every generation, renews itself by the emergence of young strangers—unknown young people who, because they have, perhaps, the scholarly perceptions of an Alexander Bickel or the social vision of a Thurgood Marshall, are able to assume positions of public responsibility and to help new generations recover and renew those values essential to our collective well-being.

As all of us who are teachers look out each fall on a new classroom of earnest faces, we are constantly aware of the possibility—indeed, we are haunted by it—that there may be sitting before us, as once there was before some other teacher, a young stranger, Abraham Lincoln; or a young stranger, Eleanor Roosevelt; or a young stranger, Martin Luther King, Jr.; or a young stranger, Alexander M. Bickel; or a young stranger, Thurgood Marshall.

A college must strive to empower its young strangers with those qualities necessary for them to assume positions of leadership in our society. It must seek to develop in these young strangers what Saul Bellow has called "an open channel to the soul"—so that the informed vigor of their public leadership will be tempered by the quiet lessons of their private contemplation.

But no college can do that job alone. Its achievement demands a commitment from each of its students to undertake a set of public responsibilities that will make this world a more just, more civilized place in which to live. It demands a commitment from each of them to cultivate a sector of privacy that will permit them to grow in understanding and sympathy. And it demands a commitment from each of them to establish a creative balance, a nurturing dialogue, between their public self and their private self, so that in the end these selves connect and a whole person emerges. It is then that they will have met the great challenge that Thomas Mann identified. They will have learned to burst the cocoon and get into the open.

The Power of Idealism

This is the first generation to enter college after the collapse of Communism and the end of the cold war. My generation, by contrast, attended college when the cold war was most menacing, when the Soviet Union threatened the interests of the United States around the world, and when the domestic search for subversion produced the political cancer of McCarthyism.

The heroes of that era of protracted confrontation were those statesmen who sought to manage the hostility between the United States and the Soviet Union and to negotiate the perils of nuclear conflict—leaders like Harry S. Truman, Winston Churchill, and George F. Kennan. Now, in the post–cold war era, as new models of heroism emerge to fit different challenges, I find myself wondering who this generation's heroes will be.

The question is not an idle one, because whom we choose for heroes speaks volumes about the aspirations and temper of our time. Heroes are signposts to a generation's ideals. By the power of their example, heroes help to mold the character of individuals and to inspire the actions of nations.

It is important to choose our heroes with care, for they will be the emblems of what we seek to emulate. They speak to what kind of persons we wish to be, what qualities of character we hope most to achieve. None of us can do the essential work of a lifetime—to consider the world thoughtfully and to contribute to it effectively—until we have earned a sense of who we are and what we seek to be.

After several generations of cold war leaders who were perforce tough-minded realists, perhaps now we are prepared for an era of leaders who are idealists. The term *idealist* is an old-fashioned one—defining a person who seeks what Yeats called "perfection of the life, or of the work"—but the need for men and women with the capacity to elevate our sights and ennoble our efforts is as timely as our most recent moment of personal doubt or despair.

An idealist whose achievements make him a hero in my own life is the playwright Václav Havel, who was the president of Czechoslovakia for almost three years—from December 1989, when his compatriots rallied in

111

Wenceslas Square and summoned him to office during a time of national exhilaration, until July 1992, when his ethnically divided nation set out on a course of creating separate Czech and Slovak states.

Born in Prague in 1936, Havel worked briefly in a chemical laboratory while preparing himself for a life in the theater, first as critic and later as playwright. Several of his plays, especially *The Garden Party, The Memorandum, A Private View,* and *The Increased Difficulty of Concentration,* have been translated into many languages and performed around the world. Havel's plays bear the special moral qualities of one who has observed with ironic wit the absurdities of political orthodoxy and the gibberish of bureaucratic hypocrisy. Tom Stoppard, the Czech-born British playwright, captured the nature of Havel's imaginative intelligence when he described his work as "absurdities pushed to absurdity compounded by absurdity and yet saved from mere nonsense by their internal logic; and, not least, the playfulness with which it is done, the almost gentle refusal to indulge a sense of grievance, the utter lack of righteousness or petulance or bile."

When, in August 1968, the reforms of the Prague Spring were crushed by Soviet tanks, Havel broadcast to his compatriots, from an underground radio station, an urgent plea for resistance. While many other writers and artists chose to collaborate with the Communist dictatorship, Havel did not, and for the next twenty years he vigorously opposed the totalitarian domination of his country.

His criticism of the Communist government for its suppression of human freedoms resulted in the banning of his plays, revocation of his passport, and repeated prison sentences. Despite this persecution, Havel became the principal spokesperson for a coalition of intellectuals, artists, and underground priests. In 1977, the coalition issued Charter 77, a human rights declaration that called on the Czech government to comply with the Helsinki Covenant on Civil and Political Rights, to which it was a signatory. Soon after the document was issued, Havel was sentenced to prison for "subversion of the Republic"—the crime of questioning the official dictum that the state can do no wrong.

By December 1989, when the so-called Velvet Revolution succeeded in throwing off Communist rule, Havel's longtime status as a dissident had given him a moral stature that stamped him as a symbol of civic courage and fresh ideas. As a result, he was catapulted into the presidency. Some saw him as a Platonic philosopher-king. Although Havel had not sought the office, he agreed to assume the role that events had written for him: he became the leader who would establish a pluralistic democracy in Czechoslovakia. He did that and more. He negotiated the withdrawal of Soviet troops from Czechoslovakia. He encouraged the nations of the Warsaw

Pact to support the reunification of Germany. He denounced anti-Semitism on a visit to Israel designed "to correct an historic wrong."

The manner in which Havel reacted to his new prominence is morally instructive. From the very outset of his presidency, Václav Havel spoke as an idealist, as an honest man with the courage to tell unpopular truths. He told his fellow citizens, for example, that they must accept responsibility for the moral illness that infected the public discourse of the Czechoslovak nation. He said that Czechs had "become accustomed to saying one thing and thinking another" and "have learned not to believe in anything, not to have consideration for one another, and only to look after ourselves. Notions such as love, friendship, compassion, humility, and forgiveness have lost their depth and dimension."

Archibald MacLeish wrote of Hemingway, derisively, that "Fame became of him." By contrast, fame did not become of Havel, nor did power seduce him. After he lost a devastating parliamentary vote on preserving the Czechoslovak union, Havel accepted the people's verdict and acknowledged that his period in power—a total of 935 days—was at a close. Like Cincinnatus, Havel relinquished power as gracefully and unpretentiously as he had assumed it. He even ventured, "I dare say I could be far more useful to my country somewhere else, whether in the theater, the press, or some benevolent institution." Standing securely on the rock of his idealism, he did not need worldly authority or ceremonial pomp to shore up his identity.

Central to Václav Havel's life—both as a private and a public person—has been a commitment to personal responsibility: the moral obligation of individuals to serve others and to recognize "the special radioactive power of the truthful word." In an arresting speech to a joint session of the United States Congress in 1990, he argued that politics was ultimately about the choices that individual men and women make—not choices to exercise individual rights, but choices to accept individual moral responsibility. "The salvation of this human world lies nowhere else than in the human heart," Havel said, "in the human power to reflect, in human meekness, and in human responsibility. . . . We are still incapable of understanding that the only genuine backbone of all our actions, if they are to be moral, is responsibility. Responsibility to something higher than my family, my country, my company, my success."

Havel's capacity for stating moral truths in political terms has instructed us that the language of democratic leaders does not need to be fitted to sound bites or targeted at some lowest common denominator. When Havel asserts that "decency and courage make sense, that something must be risked in the struggle against dirty tricks," his words engage our imagination. When Havel writes that "those who find themselves in politics therefore bear a heightened responsibility for the moral state of society," his words resonate in our souls. His eloquence reminds us that political leaders can command an audience even when they speak at length and with subtlety, so long as they have something compelling and honest to say.

There are other lessons, too, that may be drawn from Havel's example: that a respect for the power of language can breed a simple eloquence more mighty than armies; that leaders of modern nations who write their own speeches, rather than permitting others to do it for them, are much more likely to tell their fellow citizens the truth; that in mature men and women, conscience, morality, and idealism are of a piece.

For all his achievements, Havel is a man of perplexing contradictions—a combination of attractive virtues and commonplace flaws: shy but driven, ethical but manipulative, profound but self-deprecating, poetic but pragmatic, open to the views of others but stubborn in his commitment to his own. As Carl Sandburg once said in assessing the moral complexity of Lincoln, Havel is as "hard as rock and as soft as drifting fog."

Those admirers in Prague who took to calling him "Saint Václav" after the city's literary patron doubtless intended to express their appreciation of his embodiment of the Greek conception of *areté*—virtue through excellence. But they overstated the case by failing to appreciate that Havel was merely idealistic, not perfect.

If it is true, as Edmund Burke wrote, that "example is the school of mankind; they will learn at no other," Václav Havel is an elevating example of an idealist who taught the world that intellectuals possess the stuff of political responsibility and personal greatness. Indeed, in all of contemporary politics, I know of no better example than Václav Havel of the civilizing force and transcendent power of the liberal arts.

Who could have foretold, when Václav Havel was eighteen years old, that he held in the smithy of his soul such potential for greatness? Who could have foretold then that, by virtue of his idealism and self-discipline, he would one day make a hallowing contribution not only to literature but also to freedom? Who can be certain now that some of today's students—even as they feel young, untested, and apprehensive about what lies in store—may not come, through hard work and destiny, to make contributions to society that equal those of Václav Havel? Few of their contemporaries stand in so auspicious a position to advance the human condition by idealism. Few have been granted talent and privilege in such generous measure as they have. What they make of that talent, what they do with that privilege, is a test of character. Meeting that test is one of life's most satisfying achievements.

The Value of Intellectuals

The peoples of the Soviet Union, Poland, Hungary, East Germany, Czechoslovakia, Romania, and the Baltic nations have recently wrought a renaissance in the ancient values of political democracy and individual liberty. They have done so with stunning swiftness and an irresistible sense of purpose. What are the lessons that graduates of a liberal arts college can learn from this astonishing achievement?

The totalitarian governments that seized authority over Eastern Europe at the close of World War II understood all too well that language—written language, spoken language, literary language, ordinary language—is the primary instrument of democratic values. Darkly, they recognized that when language is left unfettered to speak the truth, it threatens the dogmatic discipline of authoritarian rule. Those governments shackled the honest use of language and prohibited political discourse. They brought to life the disfigured vision of Orwell's *Nineteen Eighty-Four*.

When governments forbid their people to speak their thoughts, they usurp language to their own brutal and deceitful purposes: to brazen assertion rather than sensitive speculation, to flabby glorification rather than careful skepticism, to swaggering braggadocio rather than measured nuance and intimate precision. When language is condemned to lie unexercised, it loses its hold on truth.

As the governments of Eastern Europe enforced their tyrannies of thought, they denied to several generations of people the freedom to preserve the vitality of language. Soon, language descended into a vehicle, in the words of George Steiner, for "totalitarian lies and cultural decay," for "murderous falsehoods" and hollow vulgarities.

But language did not descend unto death. In the end, as we have discovered anew, all of the totalitarian attempts to suffocate language could not suppress the idea of freedom. In country after country, the democratic revolutions in Eastern Europe have demonstrated the transforming power of language and established still again its historic connection to political freedom. The leaders of these revolutions have instructed us in the uses of language in politics. They have shown us, by the clarity of their eloquence,

that language counts in the affairs of men and women—and most powerfully when it expresses democratic truths.

No one in recent times has invoked language more strikingly to state
the theme of freedom than Václav Havel, for whose idealism I have
already expressed my admiration. In a series of riveting addresses delivered when he was president of Czechoslovakia, Havel employed language
to vault over the banality of governmental hypocrisy and to gain the elevated ground of conscience and idealism.

Four months after his release from prison, two months after his election as president, Havel told the United States Congress:

> The salvation of this human world lies nowhere else than in the
> human heart, in the human power to reflect, in human meekness, and
> in human responsibility. . . . We are still incapable of understanding
> that the only genuine backbone of all our actions, if they are to be
> moral, is responsibility. Responsibility to something higher than my
> family, my country, my company, my success—responsibility to the
> order of being where all our actions are indelibly recorded and where
> and only where they will be properly judged.

Who would have believed that a modern nation would choose a playwright as its president? Havel's powers of language and thought remind us
that Shelley was profoundly right when he said that "poets are the unac-
knowledged legislators of the world." Havel's example instructs us that
intellectuals *can* and *do* matter in the daily conduct of democratic affairs.
They matter because they express ideas clearly. They matter because they
are able, by the inspired use of language, to transport us to a higher van-
tage point of observation on the moral horizon of our lives.

From John Locke to Thomas Jefferson, from Boris Pasternak to
Aleksandr Solzhenitsyn, from Thomas Mann to Günter Grass, it has been
working intellectuals who have invoked the power of language to express
the resolute truths of political destiny.

Abraham Lincoln spoke in a language of biblical simplicity when he
formulated anew the meaning of democratic government and sought to
heal the awful wounds of war. Winston Churchill's Ciceronian rhetoric
rallied the indomitable spirit of the British people during the Battle of
Britain. Martin Luther King, Jr.'s ecclesiastical eloquence expressed for all
time the undeniable claim of equality on the realization of the American
dream.

The recent rebirth of democratic values in Eastern Europe thus
reflects a larger historical pattern—the power of language and the role of
intellectuals in recovering and preserving political freedom. From Abra-

ham Lincoln to Martin Luther King, Jr., from Winston Churchill to Václav Havel, leaders with a command of language and thought have inspired their fellow citizens to hold fast to their moral bearings.

The actions of Václav Havel summon us to recognize that intellectuals have obligations, by virtue of their capacities of language and thought, to the destinies of their fellow citizens. In accepting the call to political responsibility that his nation issued, Václav Havel recognized that at certain moments intellectuals must become persons of public power, that at critical junctures persons of thought must become persons of political responsibility.

In his speech before Congress, Havel praised Thomas Jefferson for writing the Declaration of Independence. He went on to say, "What gave meaning to that act, however, was the fact that the author backed it up with his life. It was not just his words; it was his deeds as well." Havel then spoke of himself:

> I am not the first, nor will I be the last, intellectual to do this. On the contrary, my feeling is that there will be more and more of them all the time. If the hope of the world lies in human consciousness, then it is obvious that intellectuals cannot go on forever avoiding their share of responsibility for the world and hiding their distaste for politics under the alleged need to be independent.

Havel would doubtless acknowledge that the value of intellectuals can be overstated. But a country like ours—a country that, as Richard Hofstadter once commented, has made anti-intellectualism "a familiar part of our national vocabulary of self-recrimination and intramural abuse"—hardly faces a clear or present danger of overvaluing the participation of intellectuals in public affairs. Our obligation is to appreciate that when creative minds join language and thought to the pragmatic arts of statecraft, they can transform the quality of public life.

And so, I propose a quiet salute to those dedicated intellectuals who, like Václav Havel, place their gifts of mind and language in the service of democratic government. They teach us, by their example, that liberal education seeks to preserve the humane values of freedom and to encourage individual responsibility for the common good. For that, they deserve our great gratitude.

Insiders and Outsiders

The story of Jewish leadership in American society, and specifically of a half-century of Jewish leadership on the Supreme Court of the United States, plays out the title of a poem by Archibald MacLeish: "America Is Promises." From the very beginning, America has indeed been promises, often cast in the form of bold assertions, starting with the statement in the Declaration of Independence that "all men are created equal."

What has distinguished this nation from virtually every other country in the world has been the nobility of its promises and (with some inexcusable exceptions) the strength of its national commitment to keeping them. Success in honoring this commitment depends in part on America's capacity to produce inspired leaders.

If de Tocqueville was correct when he wrote, in the 1830s, that the American aristocracy "is not among the rich, who are united by no common tie, but . . . it occupies the judicial bench and the bar," then a significant number of Jewish lawyers have been a part of that aristocracy. In an unbroken succession extending for fifty-three years—from Woodrow Wilson's appointment of Louis Dembitz Brandeis in 1916, through the appointments of Benjamin N. Cardozo in 1932, Felix Frankfurter in 1939, and Arthur J. Goldberg in 1962, to the resignation of Abe Fortas in 1969—five Jews served as justices of the United States Supreme Court. During six of those fifty-three years, from 1932 to 1938, Justice Brandeis and Justice Cardozo served as colleagues; and during the first month of his tenure, Justice Frankfurter served with Justice Brandeis.

Because of the long duration of their respective tenures, it is useful to focus primarily on Justices Brandeis and Frankfurter, and especially on their success in negotiating the perilous borderland between the formal commands of the law and the personal ideals that grew out of their own individual experiences, on the role that their Jewish identities may have played in the discharge of their judicial responsibilities, and on the meaning of their legacies to a tradition that seeks to preserve America as a nation of promises.

Benjamin N. Cardozo, speaking in 1931 at the Jewish Institute of

119

Religion, described one of the indispensable elements of a true moral leader:

> The submergence of self in the pursuit of an ideal, the readiness to spend oneself without measure, prodigally, almost ecstatically, for something intuitively apprehended as great and noble, spend oneself one knows not why—some of us like to believe that this is what religion means.

The lives of Justices Brandeis and Frankfurter bear forceful witness to Justice Cardozo's ethical imperative to associate one's efforts with a cause larger than one's self. As two of the most important legal figures of this century, Brandeis and Frankfurter were idealists, intellectuals, and powerful spokesmen for the philosophy of judicial restraint—Brandeis, the "people's advocate," pursuing social justice and the right to privacy; Frankfurter, the Harvard Law School professor and presidential counselor, devising new theories of federal jurisdiction and constitutional adjudication. What role did their Jewish identities play in the character and texture of their judicial achievements?

Louis D. Brandeis was born in Louisville, Kentucky, in 1856, to immigrant parents of Bohemian origin. His early life was one of virtual assimilation into the mainstream of American culture. His family "wore their Jewishness lightly," in the words of Robert A. Burt, author of a fascinating study of Brandeis and Frankfurter entitled *Two Jewish Justices: Outcasts in the Promised Land*. Although Brandeis's parents did not deny their Jewish identity, neither did they choose to attend synagogue, to provide their children with religious instruction, or to observe the holy days.

In his book *The Jews in America*, Arthur Hertzberg has placed a turning point of Brandeis's life in 1910, when he came to know Eastern European Jews engaged in a bitter garment workers strike. He was deeply impressed by these poorly educated immigrants, in whom he found "in a striking degree the qualities which, to my mind, make for the best American citizenship, . . . a true democratic feeling and a deep appreciation of the elements of social justice." Brandeis came to believe that these immigrants from Eastern Europe embodied "the age-old ideals of the Jews," which he asserted were identical to "the twentieth-century ideals of America."

Three years later, in 1913, at a more public turning point in his life, Brandeis abandoned the comfort of his assimilated status and embraced the cause of Zionism—until then almost entirely a movement of Eastern European immigrants, especially Russian Jews. For most German Jews, who desired to be seen as Americans of the Jewish faith rather than as members of a separate people, Zionism was an acutely embarrassing phenomenon.

Hertzberg argues that Brandeis was an "alienated aristocrat" and that his willingness to assume leadership of the Zionist movement may have been motivated, consciously or not, by his anger at the established German Jewish leaders who, he believed, had counseled President Wilson not to appoint him secretary of the interior, because he was a Progressive and a radical whose appointment might fuel the fires of anti-Semitism—that is, he was an outsider. In any event, Brandeis gave the Zionist movement the mainstream respectability that the German Jewish community had denied it, and in return the Zionist movement conferred on Brandeis an identification with the morality of Judaism that he previously had wanted.

In 1916 Wilson nominated Brandeis to be a justice of the United States Supreme Court. The primary constitutional issue of Brandeis's era was the tension between the states' exercise of police power to protect workers and consumers from exploitation in the marketplace and the states' constitutional obligation to respect property rights and freedom of contract. On the Court, Justice Brandeis normally voted to uphold state laws enacted under the police power, not because he always agreed with the substantive wisdom of these laws, but rather because he believed that the Supreme Court ought to defer to reasonable exercises of state legislative judgment. Thus, he usually dissented from the Court's invalidation of state laws as violative of the Fourteenth Amendment's due-process clause. For Brandeis, when the Supreme Court set itself up as an agency to check social and economic experimentation by the states, it ran the risk of erecting the justices' transient personal prejudices into inviolate principles of constitutional law.

Of the hundreds of decisions in which Justice Brandeis participated during his twenty-three-year tenure on the Court, one is of particular interest. In *Meyer v. Nebraska* (1923), Justice Brandeis joined the opinion of the Court holding that a Nebraska law forbidding German-language instruction in elementary schools was unconstitutional. Because Brandeis did not write an opinion of his own, we do not know why he voted, uncharacteristically, to strike down a state law on substantive grounds.

We do know that, the next summer, he told Professor Frankfurter that as long as the conservative justices who formed a majority on the Court prevailed in using the due-process clause not merely to guarantee procedural regularity but also to protect property rights, he felt it appropriate to extend the same conceptual protection to "the right to your education [and] to utter speech." But it may be that deeper, more personal reasons were at play. The Nebraska law, enacted immediately after World War I, derogated the status of the German-speaking minority in Nebraska.

Brandeis's own family had spoken German at home, and he himself had attended a German-speaking school in Louisville. Is it possible, then, as Burt suggests, that Brandeis's vote in *Meyer v. Nebraska* reflects "an instinctive sympathy with oppressed outsiders"?

Professor Burt emphasizes that Brandeis's sentiments stood in sharp contrast to those of most of his colleagues on the Court. Brandeis believed that his more conservative brethren, coming from comfortable personal backgrounds, found it virtually impossible to "admit the reality of the other fellow's predicament." He took it on himself to "enrich [their] knowledge and enlarge [their] understanding" of the common man's point of view and to teach them that economic regulations protecting consumers and employees were usually reasonable exercises of a state's legislative authority.

Brandeis's decisions during a long career stem not only from a philosophy of judicial self-restraint and not only from a firm belief that the purpose of jurisprudence is social justice. They stem also from an unshakable conviction, Old Testament in its character, of the existence of ultimate standards of justice. As law clerk to Justice Brandeis, Dean Acheson once mischievously provoked a visitor to assert the relativist notion "that moral principles were no more than generalizations from the morés or accepted notions of a particular time and place." Acheson details the predictably explosive reaction that followed:

> The Justice wrapped the mantle of Isaiah around himself, dropped his voice a full octave, jutted his eyebrows forward in a most menacing way, and began to prophesy. Morality was truth; and truth had been revealed to man in an unbroken, continuous, and consistent flow by the great prophets and poets of all time. He quoted Goethe in German and from Euripides via Gilbert Murray. On it went—an impressive, almost frightening, glimpse of an elemental force.

For Brandeis, this "mantle of Isaiah" was interwoven with a passionate disdain for large-scale economic enterprises—what he called the "curse of bigness"—and a devotion to the Jeffersonian ideals of decentralized democracy and liberating reason.

Zionism was entirely consistent with his conception of American patriotism. In 1920 Brandeis decided not to resign from the Court to assume the presidency of the American delegation at the World Zionist Congress, explaining that if he retired from the bench, critics would say "that a man cannot be a Zionist and a good citizen of his country because there was Brandeis, who was supposed to be one of the most American of

Americans who left his court and his country at the time that many will believe to be its greatest need."

Even as Brandeis's Jewish background affected his role as a justice and as an American, so his faith in America informed his attitude toward Zionism. He envisioned Palestine as an idealized version of Jeffersonian democracy, a nation of independent yeomen-farmers that would recall the United States back to the aspirations of the Founders. This, according to Burt, is what Brandeis meant when he said, in 1914, "To be good Americans, we must be better Jews, and to be better Jews we must become Zionists."

The life of Justice Brandeis reflects the ways in which an insider status as judge and an outsider status as Jew can combine to form the basis of a distinguished career of leadership. In the life of Felix Frankfurter, whom President Roosevelt appointed to the Supreme Court in 1939, insider and outsider status combined to produce a career that stands in significant contrast to that of Brandeis.

Unlike Brandeis, who was born in the United States, Frankfurter came to this country from Vienna at the age of twelve. He was forbidden to speak German in school. He was forced to adopt American ways. He grew up as an observant Jew and continued in the faith until, as a junior at the City College of New York, he concluded that the ritual no longer held any meaning for him—at which point, as he records in his diary, he left in the middle of a Yom Kippur service, "never to return."

If in his adult years Frankfurter no longer expressed his Jewish identity through faithful observance, he did so zealously through political activism. He followed Brandeis into the Zionist movement and, after Brandeis's elevation to the Court, acted as his agent in Jewish affairs. At Harvard, Frankfurter battled against quotas for Jews in the admission of students and in faculty hiring, and he opposed the association of the university with Nazi-controlled institutions in Germany. He lobbied his friend President Roosevelt for a forthright condemnation of Nazi policies against Jews, and he worked tirelessly to find places for refugee Jewish intellectuals in American universities. In all these activities, Frankfurter was expressing not only his Jewish identity but also his supreme faith in America's promises. "If one faith can be said to unite a great people," he said, "surely the ideal that holds us together beyond any other is our belief in the moral worth of the common man, whatever his race or religion. In this faith America was founded, to this faith have her poets and seers and statesmen and the unknown millions, generation after generation, devoted their lives."

In January 1939, Frankfurter sent Roosevelt the first of many notes to him written on Supreme Court stationary. It was a note from an immigrant who had become an American insider. "Dear Frank," he wrote, "In the mysterious ways of Fate, the Duchess County American and the Viennese American have for decades pursued the same directions of devotion to our beloved country. And now, on your blessed birthday I am given the gift of opportunity for service to the Nation which, in any circumstances would be owing, but which I would rather have had at your hands than at those of any other president barring Lincoln."

For Frankfurter, unlike for Brandeis, being an American meant casting off entirely old definitions of one's self in order to adopt new ones. From the large number of his Supreme Court decisions, four opinions are especially illustrative of the tension he must have felt as an insider justice and an outsider Jew.

In *Schneiderman v. United States* (1943), Frankfurter joined a dissenting opinion that argued that the United States had the constitutional authority to set aside the citizenship of a naturalized citizen on the ground that he was an active member of the Communist Party at the time he was naturalized. In connection with his dissent, Frankfurter wrote tellingly in his diary, "As one who has no ties with any formal religion, perhaps the feelings that underlie religious forms for me run into intensification of my feelings about American citizenship." Frankfurter's insistence on a narrow Americanism seems strikingly different from the views of Brandeis, who saw in the unacculturated Eastern European Jewish immigrants, as Hertzberg writes, "better Americans than the impeccably 'American' Jewish bourgeoisie into which he had been born."

In *Trop v. Dulles* (1958), the Court held unconstitutional a federal statute that removed the citizenship of any member of the armed forces convicted by court-martial of wartime desertion. In elaborating the Court's view that the statute imposed a cruel and unusual punishment forbidden by the Eighth Amendment, Chief Justice Warren wrote:

> There may be involved no physical mistreatment, no primitive torture. There is instead the total destruction of the individual's status in organized society. . . . His very existence is at the sufferance of the country in which he happens to find himself. While any one country may accord him some rights, . . . no country need do so because he is stateless. Furthermore, his enjoyment of even the limited rights of an alien might be subject to termination at any time by reason of deportation. In short, the expatriate has lost the right to have rights.

However, Frankfurter, pleading for judicial restraint, dissented. He argued that although the punishment of becoming an alien in one's own land was severe, statelessness need not lead to arbitrary treatment—"not while this Court sits." Despite the harsh consequences of statelessness, Frankfurter placed adherence to patriotic duty and loyalty to one's country at the center of his pantheon of American values.

In 1940, as headlines daily proclaimed repeated acts of Nazi aggression, the Supreme Court decided *Minersville School District v. Gobitis*, upholding the constitutionality of a statute requiring all students, including the children of Jehovah's Witnesses, to salute the flag. Jehovah's Witnesses considered saluting the flag to be the sacrilege of worshiping a graven image. Chief Justice Hughes assigned the majority opinion to Frankfurter, he later recalled, because of Frankfurter's emotional description, in conference, of the "role of the public school in instilling love of country," based on his own experiences as an immigrant child. In his opinion for the Court, Frankfurter wrote that "national unity is the basis of national security," and he emphasized that such unity is fostered by symbols.

When the Supreme Court took the unusual step of reversing itself just three years later, in *West Virginia State Board of Education v. Barnette* (1943), Justice Jackson's majority opinion alluded to the coercive tactics of the totalitarian enemies that America was then fighting. It condemned compulsory governmental measures designed to achieve uniformity of opinion. Frankfurter, in dissent, was unrepentant. In one of the most confessional and emotional of Supreme Court opinions, he wrote:

> One who belongs to the most vilified and persecuted minority in history is not likely to be insensible to the freedoms guaranteed by our Constitution. Were my purely personal attitude relevant, I should wholeheartedly associate myself with the general libertarian views in the Court's opinion, representing as they do the thought and action of a lifetime. But as judges, we are neither Jew nor Gentile, neither Catholic nor agnostic. We owe equal attachment to the Constitution and are equally bound by our judicial obligations whether we derive our citizenship from the earliest or the latest immigrants to these shores.

With respect to his *Barnette* dissent, questions remain: How much was Frankfurter guided by his academic philosophy of judicial restraint? How much by his personal conviction that national security necessitated national unity? How much by his idealistic belief that cultural outsiders must sometimes conform their behavior to majority practices? Frankfurter's dismissal of the religious convictions of Jehovah's Witnesses was a far cry from Brandeis's effort "to appreciate [the other person's] point of view."

Frankfurter had come to the Supreme Court in 1939 with every expectation, both on his part and President Roosevelt's, that he would quickly establish himself as an insider—as the Court's moral and intellectual leader. As a professor at Harvard Law School, he had been an inspirational teacher whose example encouraged many of the brightest of his students to enter public service; in public life, he had been one of the first scholars to serve as an intimate advisor to a president of the United States, and he had been a catalytic agent of the New Deal.

But Frankfurter had found that the Court was not for swaying. Justices of the stature and independence of Hugo L. Black, William O. Douglas, and Robert H. Jackson, to name only three, did not take kindly to Frankfurter's tendency to lecture them as if they were his law students. Antagonisms developed further when Frankfurter's views on judicial restraint and federalism came into conflict with Black's passionate belief that the due-process clause of the Fourteenth Amendment incorporated the Bill of Rights, making its provisions applicable to the states. Frankfurter took Black's philosophical opposition as a personal affront. As Black's influence over his colleagues widened, Frankfurter attributed to his opponents on the Court the most cynical of self-seeking motives. "In the service of this bitter vision," Burt writes, "Frankfurter repeatedly isolated himself on the Court with an almost perverse willfulness."

Frankfurter did, of course, become one of the most influential jurists of the twentieth century, and for nearly a quarter of a century he was the Court's chief exponent of judicial restraint. But for all his brilliance, something in Justice Frankfurter's makeup kept him from realizing, during his long tenure on the Supreme Court, his fullest potential for leadership. Burt suggests that Frankfurter's shortcomings as a leader may have stemmed from an immigrant son's inability to reconcile his desire to be an insider with his feelings that, as a Jew, his destiny was perpetually to be an outsider.

Frankfurter died in 1965 on Washington's birthday. He was eighty-two. Among the one hundred people who gathered for the memorial service at the Frankfurters' apartment were the president of the United States and the Supreme Court justices. Louis Henkin, a former law clerk, read the Mourner's Prayer in Hebrew. (Frankfurter had insisted, "I came into the world a Jew and I want to leave it as a Jew.") Paul Freund, Brandeis's law clerk and Frankfurter's friend, read—as Frankfurter had read at the service for Brandeis—the section from *The Pilgrim's Progress* that speaks of the death of Mr. Valiant-for-Truth: "My sword I give to him that shall succeed me in my pilgrimage, and my courage and skill to him that can get it. My marks and scars I carry with me, to be a witness for me that I have fought his battles who now will be my rewarder."

When de Tocqueville wrote of the leadership of lawyers in the 1830s,

Jews made up only a minuscule fraction of the legal profession. A century later, Brandeis foresaw the opening to Jews of a path to leadership in the law. As he wrote to Frankfurter in 1929:

> There is in the Jew a certain potential spirituality and sense of public service which can be more easily aroused and directed than at present is discernible in American non-Jews. The difficulty which the Law Schools now have in getting able men may offer opportunities, not open in other fields of intellectual activity.

The accuracy of Brandeis's assessment of new opportunities in academic life may be gauged by the fact that today Jews comprise as much as half of the faculties in elite law schools and hold a substantial number of law school deanships.

In the legal profession, as in other upper-middle-class occupations in America, Jews are now virtually indistinguishable from non-Jews in the goals they pursue. As Daniel J. Elazar has suggested in *Community and Polity: The Organizational Dynamics of American Jewry*, "most American Jews of the generation that has emerged since 1950 accept their Jewish birth as a matter of course" and are likely to be "as secularist as the most secular elements in American society."

Among American Jews of the 1990s, I wonder how much remains of what Brandeis described as "a certain potential spirituality and sense of public service." I wonder how fully Cardozo's ideal of selfless leadership can be realized among Jews who are now deeply immersed in an American culture that—to quote de Tocqueville once more—"leads men to a kind of virtuous materialism, which would not corrupt, but enervate, the soul, and noiselessly unbend its springs of action." I wonder how many of our children's generation, born to the comforts of their parents' financial successes, will respond to the urgent summons to public leadership that called forth the idealism and intellectual talents of such Jews as Brandeis and Frankfurter.

This is not a time for Americans to pull back in our efforts to redeem the promise of equality. Rather, it is a time for our nation's leaders to speak out in support of America's promises. It is a time to counsel idealism, not cynicism; generosity, not narrow self-interest. It is a time to recall, in the words of the philosopher Henri Bergson, "the tone and accents of the Prophets of Israel. It is their voice we hear when a great injustice has been done and condoned. From the depths of the centuries they raise their protest."

In working to extend equal opportunities to all Americans, American Jews today respond to "the tone and accents of the Prophets of Israel." We demonstrate our awareness that we have a responsibility to provide the public leadership of the insider and the private moral perspective of the outsider. By serving as both models of national citizenship and idealistic critics of public policy, we will prove heirs to the tradition of Brandeis and Frankfurter in ensuring that America endures as a nation of promises.

Thurgood Marshall: Man of Character

In the years ahead, significant volumes of biography and history will undoubtedly enlarge our understanding of Thurgood Marshall's skill as an advocate and his stature as a judge. I want, instead, to consider Justice Marshall as a man of character.

In 1742, Henry Fielding began *Joseph Andrews*, one of the first great English novels, with the sentence, "It is a trite but true observation that examples work more forcibly on the mind than precepts: and if this be just in what is odious and blamable, it is more strongly so in what is amiable and praiseworthy." In calling attention to the power of example to shape our respect for human achievement, Fielding performs an important service. He reminds us that exemplary lives matter. For me—as for the thousands of people, young and old, white and black, from all walks of life, who filed through the Great Hall of the Supreme Court when the justice's body lay in state in January 1993—the example of Thurgood Marshall as a person of character does truly matter and carries extraordinary power. By mastering the law, Thurgood Marshall transcended it, and thereby became an inspiring exemplar of civic virtue.

There are doubtless those who worked with Thurgood Marshall whose lives were not changed by that experience. But I have yet to meet one. All of us—his law clerks, his associates at the NAACP Legal Defense and Educational Fund, Inc., and his colleagues at the Justice Department, on the United States Court of Appeals for the Second Circuit, and on the United States Supreme Court—were marked indelibly by Justice Marshall's idealism and courage, his compassion and humanity, his craftsmanship and wit. The force of his moral example changed our lives utterly, and in ways that have made us better citizens and more reflective lawyers.

If this nation had an equivalent to Plutarch's *Lives*—a set of commentaries on men and women who had lived instructive and noble lives— an essay on Thurgood Marshall would surely be included. It would capture and memorialize the essential qualities of Marshall's character—his physical courage, his intellectual brilliance and professional expertise, his moral strength, and his utter disregard for fame and wealth. It would explore, above all, the beliefs that anchored his lifetime commitment to racial and social justice.

In a lecture delivered in 1967, Thurgood Marshall argued that the history of the litigation leading up to *Brown v. Board of Education* (1954) indicated "that law can not only respond to social change but can initiate it, and that lawyers, through their everyday work in the courts, may become social reformers." Indeed, he went further in stating that lawyers "have a duty in addition to that of representing their clients; they have a duty to represent the public, to be social reformers in however small a way." That lecture states the credo of a career.

Thurgood Marshall was the child of a pragmatic American liberalism. He was an idealist who believed deeply in the rule of the law, in the power of government to improve the social and economic conditions of its citizens, and in the promise of the Declaration of Independence. He knew that idealism was the most certain foundation of immortality. Idealists are not perfect, but their examples endure.

In *The Souls of Black Folk*, published in 1903, W. E. B. Du Bois argued, in an often quoted passage, that the central issue for American blacks was the "racial two-ness" that lies at the heart of their identity. "One ever feels his two-ness," he wrote, "an American, a Negro; two souls, two thoughts, two unreconciled strivings; two warring ideals in one dark body. . . . The history of the American Negro is the history of this strife— this longing to attain self-conscious manhood, to merge his double self into a better and truer self."

Like Du Bois, Thurgood Marshall was fiercely proud to be an American and fiercely proud to be a Negro. And for Marshall, as for Du Bois, the complex fate of being an African-American was the overarching challenge of his life. Marshall's life is one of the great American stories; it is emblematic of an heroic theme: a young man from modest circumstances, confronted by racial discrimination and social hostility, contributes mightily, by the power of his mind and the strength of his character, to the redemption of his nation's highest ideals.

Born in Baltimore in 1908, the grandson of a freed slave and Union soldier, Thurgood Marshall became one of the most important public lawyers of the century (only Louis D. Brandeis belongs in his class) and the first African-American to serve as a justice of the Supreme Court. Marshall was also the first Marylander appointed to the Court since Chief Justice Roger B. Taney, author of the *Dred Scott* decision, which held that Negroes were not "citizens" and had no rights under the Constitution. Marshall's succession to the seat held by Justice Tom C. Clark, grandson of a Confederate soldier, symbolized the slow playing out of our national destiny.

Thurgood Marshall came from a proud and close-knit family; his was a privileged background, compared to many African-Americans at the beginning of the century. His mother, Norma Marshall, was a college-educated elementary-school teacher. His father, William Canfield Marshall, was a Pullman car porter and, later, a country-club steward at an all-white yacht club on Chesapeake Bay.

From his parents he derived a sense of identity, of self-worth, of destiny. He learned from them not to be bitter in the face of racial discrimination and to judge people, white and black, by their character and their achievements. Marshall loved repeating his father's remark, "Son, if anyone ever calls you a nigger, you not only got my permission to fight him—you got my orders to fight him." On a number of occasions, Marshall carried out those orders.

A democratic American with a small *d*, Marshall was not a respecter of rank. When he was introduced to Britain's Prince Philip, the Duke of Edinburgh asked, "Do you care to hear my opinion of lawyers?" Justice Marshall, mimicking the superior tones of the royal accent, replied with a disarming smile, "Only if you care to hear my opinion of princes."

After Marshall was graduated from public high school in Baltimore, his mother pawned—and did not reclaim—her wedding and engagement rings so that he could go to college. He followed his brother, Aubrey, to Lincoln University in Chester, Pennsylvania. Known as the "black Princeton" because many of its faculty were Princeton graduates, Lincoln was the nation's oldest all-black college. Among Marshall's classmates were the poet Langston Hughes, the musician Cab Calloway, and Kwame Nkrumah, the first president of Ghana.

Having received his degree from Lincoln, Marshall was rebuffed in his efforts to attend the all-white University of Maryland Law School—a ten-minute trolley ride from his home. Instead, he was forced to commute to Howard Law School in Washington, where he was graduated in 1933 as valedictorian of his class.

It was at Howard that he met the most important mentor of his life, Charles Hamilton Houston, the law school's Harvard-educated dean. Houston impressed on Marshall the obligation of eliminating segregation and taught him that "lawyers are either social engineers or parasites." Many years later, Marshall conferred a high compliment on Houston by describing him as "the engineer of it all."

Marshall declined a graduate fellowship at Harvard Law School and entered private practice in Baltimore. At twenty-four, it was time to support himself and begin his life's work of fighting segregation.

In one of his first cases after law school, working in collaboration with Houston and the NAACP, he brought suit to compel the University of

Maryland Law School to enroll its first African-American student. Winning the case, Marshall said, was "sweet revenge."

Despite this early success, Marshall's years at the Baltimore bar were difficult ones. The Depression made it virtually impossible for him to earn a living. With paying clients few and far between, he threw himself into community activities, including those of the NAACP, in order to establish his reputation as a lawyer.

Houston cautioned Marshall not to neglect the development of his own private practice for the work he was doing for the NAACP on the side. But the advice was to no avail. Marshall's attention and talents were increasingly captured by the cases he was handling for the NAACP. In 1935 Marshall told Houston, "Personally, I would not give up these cases here in Maryland for anything in the world, but at the same time there is no opportunity to get down to really hustling for business."

Marshall began to cast around for other sources of income. He applied to teach at Howard Law School, and in September 1936 he wrote to Houston, who by then had become the legal director of the NAACP, that "something must be done about money." During the prior six months, Marshall had earned less than two hundred dollars from his NAACP work, and this was virtually his entire income for the period.

When Marshall asked that he be paid a monthly retainer of $150 for his NAACP work, Houston suggested that Marshall, instead, join him on the legal staff of the NAACP in New York City. Thus, under circumstances that were hardly auspicious, Marshall moved to New York in October 1936 and began to work full-time with the NAACP—an association from which history would be made. Marshall now had the momentous opportunity to ally his formidable talents with an idea whose time had come.

Houston and Marshall complemented each other in styles, strengths, and personalities. In their biography of Marshall, *Thurgood Marshall: Warrior at the Bar, Rebel on the Bench*, Michael D. Davis and Hunter R. Clark have written, "Houston was low-key, well organized, formal in his demeanor. . . . Thurgood was the gregarious extrovert, a backslapper who quickly won friends. Houston was smart. Marshall was shrewd. Houston was the better writer, Marshall the better speaker, lacing his conversations with humor, logic, salty and streetwise language."

Two years later, in 1938, when Houston retired, Thurgood Marshall, at age thirty, became chief counsel of the NAACP, which later would establish its legal division as a separate organization, the NAACP Legal Defense and Educational Fund, Inc.

When Houston had offered Marshall the job at the NAACP, he had warned that extensive traveling would be required and that some of the travel would be dangerous. He was right on both counts. During those years—before jet planes or the interstate highway system—Marshall traveled an average of sixty thousand miles a year, mostly across the South, trying cases and establishing a network of lawyers—white and black—who were willing to take civil rights cases. Danger was always close at hand. He frequently was escorted by armed black guards. In undertaking the defense of criminal cases throughout the South, Marshall demonstrated one of the significant components of his character: physical courage.

Marshall often told of the time when he was waiting for a train in a small Mississippi town where he had investigated a lynching. Hungry, he decided to "put my civil rights in my back pocket and go to the back door of the kitchen [of a local restaurant] and see if I could buy a sandwich," he recalled. "And while I was kibitzing myself to do that, this white man came up beside me in plain clothes with a great big pistol on his hip. And he said, 'Nigger boy, what are you doing here?' And I said, 'Well, I'm waiting for the train to Shreveport.' And he said, 'There's only one more train that comes through here, and that's the four o'clock, and you'd better be on it because the sun is never going down on a live nigger in this town.'" Marshall concluded: "Guess what? I was on that train."

Another component of Marshall's character was his respect for intellect. He was a man who appreciated intellectuals. From the beginning of his career, he eagerly enlisted the talents of individuals more learned than practicing lawyers could hope to be. He said, "I never hesitated to pick other people's brains—brains I didn't have." The names of those members of the academic world who assisted him in the years leading up to *Brown v. Board of Education* constitute an honor roll of outstanding scholars, including Erwin N. Griswold, Walter Gellhorn, Charles L. Black, Jr., Louis H. Pollak, John Hope Franklin, C. Vann Woodward, Robert K. Carr, and Kenneth B. Clark.

In addition, Marshall had an uncanny ability to recognize legal talent. The lawyers with whom he worked over the years included Robert L. Carter, Constance Baker Motley, and Spottswood W. Robinson, III, all of whom went on to distinguished careers as federal judges, as well as William T. Coleman, Jr., and Jack Greenberg.

But Marshall's special genius lay in his ability to apply the learning of intellectuals from many fields in ways that advanced his cause dramatically. The most famous example of Marshall's practice of bringing the scholarship of others to bear on legal argument was his use of Gunnar Myrdal's comprehensive study of the Negro in the United States, *An American Dilemma*.

Published in 1944, Myrdal's book made a stunning impression on

American policymakers. It demonstrated that segregation was not only devastating to the black minority, which lived in fear of harsh and arbitrary treatment, but also deleterious to the white majority, which experienced a profound sense of moral guilt over the undeserved advantages and privileges that the accident of their race afforded them. By emphasizing the tension between the destructive impact of racial segregation on black character and culture and the nobility of America's professed ideals of liberty, justice, and equality, Myrdal's book provided compelling tactical support for undermining the doctrine of "separate but equal."

Marshall's reliance on Myrdal's work proved to be inspired. Chief Justice Warren's unanimous opinion in *Brown v. Board of Education* held that racial segregation in the public schools was unconstitutional. And the decision cited *An American Dilemma* for the proposition that separate schools are inherently unequal.

Surely *Brown v. Board of Education* was the crowning achievement of Marshall's career—either before his service on the Supreme Court or after. Had his legal career ended at that point, Marshall would have earned an important place in American history. Already he had done more than perhaps any other citizen—with the towering exception of Abraham Lincoln—to address the American dilemma of relations between the races. But Marshall went on to serve with distinction as a member of the United States Court of Appeals for the Second Circuit, as solicitor general of the United States, and for twenty-four years as a justice of the United States Supreme Court.

Marshall came to prominence at a moment when the explosion of new media of communications had fueled American society's growing preoccupation with fame. Marshall's strength of character was such that he never confused fame—or, for that matter, money—with achievement. The desire "to live in the minds of others," as Samuel Johnson said, has always been intense, but it was most particularly television that confused celebrity with authority and made it possible for a person to become, in Daniel J. Boorstin's phrase, "known for his well-knownness," rather than for accomplishments that warrant enduring recognition.

It is important to observe that Thurgood Marshall's remarkable achievements and professional eminence came, in large part, precisely *because* he had no desire to be famous for the sake of being famous. At one time, he was perhaps the most celebrated lawyer in the United States. His picture appeared on the cover of *Time* magazine. The press called him "Mr. Civil Rights." Yet Marshall's fame neither went to his head nor deflected his vision. He knew that neither fame nor fortune could provide nourishment sufficient to sustain his idealism.

Marshall's commitment was to the public profession of the law, not to the acquisition of wealth. When President Kennedy nominated him to the court of appeals in 1961, his salary at the Legal Defense Fund was $18,000. When President Johnson nominated him as solicitor general in 1965, he accepted a reduction in salary, from $33,000 to $28,500, and, perhaps more importantly, he relinquished the life tenure of a federal judge. The financial risks he took were not insignificant ones for a man concerned with supporting properly a wife and two young sons.

If President Johnson regarded Marshall's service as solicitor general as preparation for his eventual appointment as the first black justice to the Supreme Court, Marshall himself had no direct knowledge of Johnson's intentions. And he surely appreciated that the vagaries of history and politics might prevent Johnson from carrying out any intention he may then have had to name him to the Court. Despite the loss of life tenure and a reduction in salary, Marshall accepted appointment as solicitor general because his sense of responsibility to the president—and perhaps of historical destiny—outweighed his interest in financial security.

Less than two years later, President Johnson, on June 13, 1967, nominated Marshall to the Supreme Court. In making the historic announcement, Johnson said, "I believe it is the right thing to do, the right time to do it, the right man, and the right place." Justice Marshall brought unique qualifications to the Court. He was its only member who had specialized in the practice of criminal law, let alone defended dozens of men for murder and other capital crimes. He was its only member who had personally faced racial discrimination, let alone experienced the fear of being lynched when trying cases in small Southern towns. He was its only member who had successfully argued dozens of cases before the Court, let alone achieved landmark victories that expanded the meaning of the due-process and equal-protection clauses of the Fourteenth Amendment.

These unique qualifications, which helped to define Marshall's character, often found compassionate expression in his constitutional views. As Carol Steiker has said of Marshall, "He naturally understood the position of the outsider, the underdog, and the silenced, and he gave that position his powerful voice." Justice Marshall carved out a special place on the Court as a resolute defender of the constitutional rights of minorities, women, criminal defendants, the poor, the disenfranchised, the powerless.

Thus, when the Court held, in *United States v. Kras* (1973), that pauper debtors had to pay a fifty-dollar fee to file for relief in bankruptcy, Marshall took angry exception to the assertion that such debtors could save up the fee by forgoing a weekly movie or giving up two packs of cigarettes each week. "It may be easy for some people to think that weekly savings of less than $2 are no burden," Marshall wrote. "But no one who has had close contact with poor people can fail to understand how close to the margin of survival many of them are."

I do not breach a law clerk's obligation of confidentiality in recounting a story, more than thirty years after the fact, that describes one of the most powerful lessons that Judge Marshall taught me. In drafting a factual statement in a case in which an injured longshoreman had sued the owner of a cargo ship for unseaworthiness, I quoted from the plaintiff's halting testimony at trial.

Because the testimony was ungrammatical, I followed the law review practice of placing the diacritical word [sic] after several sentences. Judge Marshall took me to task. The use of the word [sic], he said sternly, might seem a useful bit of scholarly apparatus to a precocious law clerk, but it was a refined form of insult to the unlettered plaintiff and served no decisional purpose whatsoever. What was the point of that gratuitous put-down? Of course, he was right.

Justice Marshall brought to the United States Supreme Court a special—indeed, a unique—perspective. He never forgot the mean realities of life at the street level. Alone among the justices, as Robert L. Carter wrote, Justice Marshall "knew what police stations were like, what indignities emanated from rural Southern life, what the streets of New York were like, what the corrupt trial courts were like, what death sentences were like, what being black in America was like—and he knew what it felt like to be at risk as a human being." In the crucible of poverty, physical danger, injustice, and racial discrimination that taught him these mean realities, Marshall's character had been forged. The concerns of the outsider were the concerns of his lifetime. He was a "public interest lawyer" before that designation came into popular use.

Conversely, Marshall understood the opportunities he could give to minority lawyers by virtue of his position as a justice of the Supreme Court. True to his character, as he rose, he never failed to lift others. During his twenty-four years of service, Marshall chose more black and minority law clerks than any other justice, and many of these men and women now serve on the faculties of the nation's leading law schools.

He also brought to the Court a special brand of sardonic, often ironic, wit. Marshall's humor was a serious manifestation of his personality and inseparable from his strength of character. His humor was, among other things, a coping strategy; rather than a means of denying the bleakness of reality, it was a way of dealing with it and conveying it to his colleagues. Justice William J. Brennan, Jr., Marshall's closest friend on the Court, clearly recognized that Marshall's personal stories caused his colleagues to "confront walks of life we had never known."

He would resist a law clerk's assertion that he *had* to agree to a particular position by responding, "Boy, there are only two things I *have* to do: stay black and die." Similarly, he delighted in telling and retelling the story of his response to a cantankerous Southern judge who asked him, "What do you want from this court?" Said Marshall, "Anything I can get, your honor."

When I was his law clerk, I once argued a point with him too long. The judge grew impatient. Finally, he pointed to the framed document on the wall and said, "John F. Kennedy signed my commission. Who signed yours?"

When President Nixon asked Bethesda Naval Hospital to send him a full report on Justice Marshall's hospitalization for pneumonia in 1968, Marshall told the physician to put at the bottom of the file, "Not yet." His skill and charm as a storyteller remain legendary.

One of the most poignant aspects of Justice Marshall's character was the maturity with which he negotiated periods of profound disappointment as they alternated with periods of sublime satisfaction. For example, the years leading up to *Brown v. Board of Education* must have been a time of accelerating, if cautious, anticipation. Although he and his colleagues knew that the constitutional prohibition of "separate but equal" was not inevitable, they also must have sensed that it was now more likely to occur than ever previously had been the case.

Marshall could look back on his days as head of the NAACP's legal effort and see a long string of landmark victories. In *Missouri ex rel. Gaines v. Canada* (1938), the Supreme Court ordered the integration of the University of Missouri Law School. In *Morgan v. Virginia* (1946), the Court outlawed segregation on interstate buses. In *Shelley v. Kraemer* (1948), the Court barred judicial enforcement of private restrictive covenants intended to prevent the sale of houses to blacks, Jews, or members of other minority groups. And in *Sweatt v. Painter* (1950) and *McLaurin v. Oklahoma State Regents* (1950), the Court began the process of chipping away at the doctrine of "separate but equal."

Although Marshall appreciated that *Brown v. Board of Education* was a decision of surpassing historic significance, he often stated that the decision in *Smith v. Allwright* (1944), which held unconstitutional the Democratic white primary in Texas, addressed a related and perhaps equally important issue: the right to vote. Because of his deep commitment to the democratic process, Marshall placed a high value on securing for blacks the right to vote. Although the Fifteenth Amendment in 1870 had given black males the right to vote, no Southern blacks had in fact been permitted to vote before 1920, and as late as the 1940 presidential election, only 2.5 percent of eligible black voters voted in the South. When poll taxes, literacy tests, and grandfather clauses did not stop blacks from voting, threats and other forms of intimidation usually did. "Without the ballot," Marshall said, "you have no citizenship, no status, no power in this country."

Marshall's efforts and those of William H. Hastie (who would later become the first African-American appointed to a federal appeals court) to secure the voting rights of blacks forever changed the profile of city halls, state capitols, and governors' mansions. By 1993, more than 8,000 African-Americans held elected positions in the United States—including those of Governor, United States Senator, and United States Representative—compared with approximately 1,500 in 1970.

On May 17, 1954, Marshall experienced the rare satisfaction of prevailing in perhaps the most momentous case of the century. However, the heady exhilaration of winning *Brown* was followed, during the next several years, by the discouraging necessity of litigating the meaning of the Court's pronouncement that its ruling be effectuated "with all deliberate speed." The massive resistance mounted by large cities and rural communities alike, with the demagogic support of Southern governors, was tremendously dispiriting.

A similar pattern occurred in Justice Marshall's tenure on the Supreme Court. The Court that Marshall joined, it seems clear in retrospect, was an especially distinguished one. During his early years, he served with colleagues who were his intellectual and professional equals. The Court's senior members were among the most respected justices in American history—Earl Warren, Hugo L. Black, William O. Douglas, John Marshall Harlan, and William J. Brennan, Jr.

Those were the years in which Marshall was able to take gratification from his unparalleled capacity for craftsmanship. Like another great judge, Learned Hand, he had long ago learned that "it is as craftsmen that we get our satisfactions and our pay." Those were also the years in which many of the views he had long held became the law of the land. Those were his halcyon days.

That sense of professional gratification changed with the election of President Nixon in 1968 and the appointment in the years that followed of a number of justices—including two chief justices, Warren E. Burger and William H. Rehnquist—whose views were opposed to Marshall's in virtually every area that mattered to him most. As the membership of the Court became more conservative, he found himself increasingly in dissent, especially on such issues as a woman's right to privacy, which he supported, and capital punishment, which he opposed.

Still, with the steady purpose of a man of character devoted to causes

he regarded as proper in principle, he persevered. Following the appointments of Antonin Scalia in 1986 and Anthony Kennedy in 1988, Marshall's despair at the direction the Court was taking deepened. It became
more painful with the retirement in 1990 of Justice Brennan, Marshall's
closest ally and dearest friend.

Gradually, Marshall had become accustomed to—but not contented
with—writing dissents. He often said that the first question he asked
prospective law clerks was whether they would be satisfied with writing
dissents. "I agree with that old saying," he said, "that 'I love peace but I
adore a riot.' You've got to be angry to write a dissent."

Marshall saw such unanimous and resounding decisions as *Brown*
give way to innumerable five-to-four and six-to-three decisions, in which
he often was in the minority. For example, the Court's consensus on
school integration broke down in *Milliken v. Bradley* (1974), which
rejected, by a vote of five-to-four, a multidistrict integration plan that cov-
ered not only Detroit but its predominantly white suburban communities
as well. In a compelling dissent, Marshall argued that "the Court today
takes a giant step backwards. . . . Our Nation, I fear, will be ill served by
the Court's refusal to remedy separate and unequal education, for unless
our children begin to learn together, there is little hope that our people will
ever learn to live together." He continued:

> Racial attitudes ingrained in our Nation's childhood and adolescence
> are not quickly thrown aside in its middle years. But just as the incon-
> venience of some cannot be allowed to stand in the way of the rights
> of others, so public opposition, no matter how strident, cannot be
> permitted to divert this Court from the enforcement of the constitu-
> tional principles at issue in this case. Today's holding, I fear, is more
> a reflection of a perceived public mood that we have gone far enough
> in enforcing the Constitution's guarantee of equal justice than it is the
> product of neutral principles of law.

In *City of Mobile v. Bolton* (1980), the Court upheld, by a vote of six
to three, an at-large system for electing city commissioners—a system that
diluted black voting strength and had the practical result of electing only
whites. Marshall dissented, arguing that the discriminatory impact alone
of the new voting system was sufficient to violate the Constitution. He
warned, "If this Court refuses to honor our long-recognized principle that
the Constitution 'nullifies sophisticated as well as simple-minded modes of
discrimination,' . . . it cannot expect the victims of discrimination to
respect political channels of seeking redress."

Marshall's deepest convictions were aroused in cases involving the constitutionality of capital punishment. In *Gregg v. Georgia* (1976), the Court held, by a vote of seven to two, that the death penalty did not constitute cruel and unusual punishment under the Eighth Amendment. Only Justice Brennan shared Marshall's view that the death penalty was cruel and unusual punishment per se and, therefore, always unconstitutional.

In dissent after dissent thereafter, Marshall noted that death is irrevocable and makes rehabilitation impossible. The question, he said, "is not simply whether capital punishment is a deterrent, but whether it is a better deterrent than life imprisonment." He could find no such evidence. He wrote, "At times a cry is heard that morality requires vengeance to evidence society's abhorrence of [a criminal] act. But the Eighth Amendment is our insulation from our baser selves."

The rise of "reverse discrimination" cases was hardly less frustrating. When the Court issued its decision in *Regents of the University of California v. Bakke* (1978), permitting a state university to consider race among other factors in making admissions decisions, Marshall concurred in the result; but he did not accept that part of the Court's reasoning that held unconstitutional a separate admissions program for disadvantaged minorities. He wrote: "It must be remembered that, during most of the past 200 years, the Constitution as interpreted by this Court did not prohibit the most ingenious and pervasive forms of discrimination against the Negro. Now, when a State acts to remedy the effects of that legacy of discrimination, I cannot believe that this same Constitution stands as a barrier."

The acuteness of Marshall's pain and frustration comes through poignantly in his opinion in *Bakke*. Marshall continued, "The experience of Negroes in America has been different in kind, not just in degree, from that of any other ethnic groups. It is not merely the history of slavery alone but also that a whole people were marked as inferior by the law. And that mark has endured. The dream of America as the great melting pot has not been realized for the Negro; because of his skin color, he never even made it into the pot." More than sixty years after Marshall began his legal career, that statement remains, alas, painfully true.

One notes with aching sadness how large a proportion of Justice Marshall's twenty-four years on the Supreme Court was devoted to dissenting on the issues of greatest moment to him. Only the support of Justice Brennan consistently provided him ideological comfort—and the hopeful glimmer of eventual vindication by history—against the wrongheaded direction he believed the Court was taking.

In a moving tribute to Justice Marshall on his retirement, Justice Sandra Day O'Connor described once asking him how he avoided being despondent, given all the injustices he had witnessed during his lifetime. He told her the story of how he and Charles Houston had traveled to Loudon County, Virginia, to represent a black man accused of murdering a wealthy white woman and her white maid. After Marshall and Houston unsuccessfully challenged the exclusion of blacks from the jury, the man was convicted of murder by the all-white jury and sentenced to life in prison. Rather than risk the death penalty in a new trial, the accused chose not to appeal the exclusion of blacks from the jury. "You know something is wrong with the government's case," Justice Marshall told O'Connor, "when a Negro only gets life for murdering a white woman." Marshall added, "I just don't believe that guy got a fair shake. But what are you going to do? There are only two choices in life: stop and go on. You tell me, what would you pick?"

He once told a reunion of his law clerks, in a moment I will remember for the rest of my life, "The goal of a true democracy such as ours, explained simply, is that any baby born in these United States, even if he is born to the blackest, most illiterate, most unprivileged Negro in Mississippi, is, merely by being born and drawing his first breath in this democracy, endowed with the exact same rights as a child born to a Rockefeller. Of course it's not true. Of course it never will be true. But I challenge anybody to tell me that it isn't the type of goal we should try to get to as fast as we can."

His remarks reflected his sober skepticism, held until the very end of his life, about whether American society was yet prepared to grant equal rights and equal opportunity to minorities. While he retained a deep faith in the guarantees of the Constitution and in the ideals of the Declaration of Independence, he also held serious doubts about the nation's commitment to attaining those guarantees and ideals.

In 1987, as the nation was celebrating the bicentennial of the United States Constitution, Justice Marshall spoke to the annual seminar of the San Francisco Patent and Trademark Law Association. He reminded his audience that the Constitution "was defective from the start, requiring several amendments, a civil war, and momentous social transformation to attain the system of constitutional government, and its respect for the individual freedoms and human rights, we hold as fundamental today."

He bluntly addressed the hypocrisy of the first three words of the preamble, "We the People." The compromise in Philadelphia, he said, created an unprincipled "contradiction between guaranteeing liberty and justice to all, and denying both to Negroes." Moreover, "women did not gain the right to vote for over a hundred and thirty years."

Although he refused to celebrate the wisdom and sense of justice of the Framers, Justice Marshall praised the evolutionary manner in which the Constitution has remained a living document, especially by virtue of the adoption of the Fourteenth Amendment. He pointed out the striking role that legal principles have played in "determining the condition of Negroes" who "were enslaved by law, emancipated by law, disenfranchised and segregated by law; and, finally, they have begun to win equality by law."

The progress that blacks have achieved was not the result of the Founding Fathers, Marshall said, but of those men and women who came later. " 'We the People' no longer enslave, but the credit does not belong to the Framers. It belongs to those who refused to acquiesce in outdated notions of 'liberty,' 'justice,' and 'equality,' and who strived to better them."

For himself, Marshall said, "I plan to celebrate the Bicentennial of the Constitution as a living document, including the Bill of Rights and the other amendments protecting individual freedoms and human rights."

These sober reflections were doubtless not what his audience had expected, but Marshall's candor reflected the experience of a lifetime, as well as his unyielding faith that the Constitution could be made into a better document than the one framed by the Founding Fathers. By calling attention to the Constitution's defects at a time of widespread uncritical celebration of its virtues, Marshall made a case that virtually no contemporary had thought to make—perhaps because none possessed the strength of character that he did, and because none had reflected on it so profoundly as he had.

As the end of his life drew near, Justice Marshall's faith in the power of the Court to achieve racial and economic justice continued to falter. On July 4, 1992, six months before his death, Justice Marshall was given the Philadelphia Liberty Medal, which carried a prize of one hundred thousand dollars, in recognition of his contributions to the pursuit of liberty of conscience and the pursuit of freedom from oppression and deprivation. His speech that day, delivered at Independence Hall, was a ringing assertion and reaffirmation of the views of a lifetime:

> I wish I could say that racism and prejudice were only distant memories . . . and that liberty and equality were just around the bend. I wish I could say that America has come to appreciate diversity and to see and accept similarity.
>
> But as I look around, I see not a nation of unity but of division— Afro and white, indigenous and immigrant, rich and poor, educated

and illiterate. Even many educated whites and successful Negroes have given up on integration and lost hope in equality. . . .

We cannot play ostrich. Democracy cannot flourish amid fear. Liberty cannot bloom amid hate. Justice cannot take root amid rage. . . . We must go against the prevailing wind. We must dissent from the indifference. We must dissent from the apathy. We must dissent from the fear, the hatred, and the mistrust. We must dissent from a government that has left its young without jobs, education, or hope. We must dissent from the poverty of vision and the absence of moral leadership. We must dissent because America can do better, because America has no choice but to do better.

With his health failing, Justice Marshall's last days were sad ones. Yet his tenacity and his determination to defend his view of the Constitution—especially on such issues as capital punishment, privacy and abortion, and the rights of minorities and the poor—did not falter. He frequently told friends, "I was appointed for life, and I intend to serve out my term." But advancing age finally caused him to step down, in June of 1991. When asked how he wanted to be remembered, Marshall said, "He did the best he could with what he had."

Justice Marshall died on January 24, 1993. He was eighty-four. The public response to his death—measured most dramatically by the eighteen thousand persons, of all races and all backgrounds, who paid their final respects to him in the Great Hall of the Supreme Court—is testimony to the depth of his impact on the lives of ordinary Americans.

At Justice Marshall's funeral, held in Washington's National Cathedral, it was, to my mind, William T. Coleman, Jr., who best captured Marshall's legacy. "History will ultimately record," Coleman said, "that Mr. Justice Marshall gave the cloth and linen to the work that Lincoln's untimely death left undone."

As a result of his historic achievements, Thurgood Marshall changed the face of America. Although the changes have not been so swift in recent years as they were at the height of Marshall's career, progress will continue and the direction is certain. In the end, that progress toward the achievement of equality for all will be Thurgood Marshall's greatest legacy.

Thurgood Marshall's life was a unique conjunction of person and place, of talent and destiny. He was an American original, a man of character whose contributions to the Republic redeemed its most cherished values.

The Capacity of Imagination

One of Charles Dickens's most engaging novels, *Hard Times*, describes a soul-blighting philosophy of education that still, more than a century later, attracts far too many adherents.

As the novel opens, the businessman Thomas Gradgrind is haranguing the local schoolmaster on the need for a pedagogical revolution to prepare students for the new age that was then at hand. "Now, what I want is Facts," he insists. "Teach these boys and girls nothing but Facts." In Gradgrind's narrow curricular design, there is little room for ideas, for intellectual excitement, for spontaneity, or for imagination. He asserts: "You can only form the minds of reasoning animals upon Facts: nothing else will ever be of any service to them. . . . Stick to Facts, sir!"

It would be a mistake to read *Hard Times* as being merely an historical gloss on the Industrial Revolution or to see Gradgrind as no more than an absurd caricature of dullness and petty-mindedness. *Hard Times* is in truth a fictional treatise on moral education, a tract for the unsettled period of technological change in which it was written. However, in our own period of technological change, Dickens's indictment of a narrowly utilitarian philosophy of education has lost none of its relevance.

College students are confronted today with complex and confusing possibilities about the meaning of the "good life," with perplexing anxieties about achieving their fullest potential and choosing a satisfying career, and with the meretricious huckstering of affluence, avarice, and materialism. William James warned that such social circumstances all too readily give rise to "the moral flabbiness born of the exclusive worship of the bitch-goddess SUCCESS."

These circumstances are creating pressure on colleges and students, all across the nation, to concentrate on what Gradgrind, in *Hard Times*, calls for: a narrow, practical curriculum based on the acquisition of "Facts" alone—a curriculum that would shrivel the imagination and blunt the humane values of a liberal education.

Of course students should learn facts, but not the kind to which Gradgrind affixed a capital *F*. The learning of facts, to the extent that scholars can agree on what they are, is no more than a beginning. If facts are to supply meaning—and, even, wisdom—students must employ their own critical capacities to question facts skeptically, to consider facts imaginatively, to place facts in those larger contexts that will most fully illuminate their real significance.

The task of drawing meaning from facts is precisely what the great writers, philosophers, historians, and scientists have performed for centuries, and that is why the study of their lives and works is so rewarding. I especially admire Flannery O'Connor. Her life was heroic and her work is a triumphant example of the capacity of imagination to transform the inert stuff of facts into startling truths about the private and social lives of human beings.

Flannery O'Connor was a novelist, short-story writer, and essayist, a teacher of hard moral lessons. Her books do not yet appear on those "great books" lists that are fashionable in some quarters, but they inform the mind and stir the imagination in the most troubling and most satisfying of ways. She is a good reason why we should also celebrate the opening up of academic reading lists and syllabi to works by the most talented members of what Simone de Beauvoir ruefully called "the second sex."

Flannery O'Connor's life was short (she died at the age of thirty-nine) and, to most observers, uneventful. But, as Keats said of Shakespeare, she led a life of allegory—a life that reflected a determined and successful effort to triumph, by her intellectual gifts and energies, over the toughest of human odds.

Born in Savannah, Georgia, in 1925, she was reared in a devoutly Catholic household within the overwhelmingly Protestant culture of the Deep South. At age twenty she was graduated from Georgia State College for Women, where she had majored in sociology. When she entered the Writers' Workshop at the University of Iowa, she started her life's work as a writer.

On her arrival at Iowa, her manner was so shy and her Georgia accent so impenetrable that Paul Engle, the workshop's director, could comprehend little that she uttered. Fearing that an unqualified student had been referred to his program, he asked her to write down what she had said to him. She scribbled, on a small piece of paper, "My name is Flannery O'Connor. I am not a journalist. Can I come to the Writers' Workshop?" When Engle later read her work, he immediately recognized her talent. By the end of her first year at Iowa, she had published her first short story, "The Geranium," in the magazine *Accent*.

After she graduated from the Writers' Workshop, Flannery O'Connor began to publish her brilliantly crafted fiction. Her first novel, *Wise Blood*, published in 1952, was immediately recognized as a new departure in American fiction, a work belonging superficially to the Southern Gothic genre, but charged from within by the harsh, blinding radiance of an uncompromising religious vision. All of her work is filled with fierce violence and sardonic humor; it is grim, ironic, compassionate, comic, and profoundly disturbing. With each new book—*A Good Man Is Hard to Find* (1955), *The Violent Bear It Away* (1960), and the posthumously published *Everything That Rises Must Converge* (1965)—Flannery O'Connor's reputation grew.

For many readers, the religious content of her themes—especially her pursuit of the meaning of grace and the mystery of redemption—is difficult to reconcile with the selfishness and the often appalling evil of her maimed, displaced, and distorted characters, so many of whom are lost in a society almost entirely secular. Miss O'Connor's explanation is illuminating: "My own feeling is that writers who see by the light of their Christian faith will have, in these times, the sharpest eyes for the grotesque, for the perverse, and for the unacceptable."

She was deeply absorbed by the two fundamental questions of free will and the struggle for identity. "Free will," she wrote, "does not mean one will, but many wills conflicting in one man. Freedom cannot be conceived simply. It is a mystery and one which a novel, even a comic novel, can only be asked to deepen." Yet Flannery O'Connor also wrote about the more familiar dilemmas of daily life—the painful tensions between the generations, the quiet desperation that grows out of frustration and anger, and the insecurity of those who do not fit easily into society's conventional niches. She portrayed these existential circumstances with a stunning accuracy and economy of language.

For example, one of her characters, in "Good Country People," cannot come to terms with her mother's expectations:

> The girl had taken the Ph.D. in philosophy and this left Mrs. Hopewell at a complete loss. You could say, "My daughter is a nurse," or "My daughter is a schoolteacher," or even, "My daughter is a chemical engineer." You could not say, "My daughter is a philosopher." That was something that had ended with the Greeks and Romans. All day Joy sat on her neck in a deep chair, reading. Sometimes she went for walks but she didn't like dogs or cats or birds or flowers or nature or nice young men. She looked at nice young men as if she could smell their stupidity.

For Flannery O'Connor, writing was not a process of simply describing facts. Rather, it was a process of understanding the subtle, surprising, even bizarre relationships among unexpected juxtapositions of facts. And even more, it was a process of understanding the relationships of those patterns of facts to larger visions of life. In her case, that meant "the conflict between an attraction for the Holy and the disbelief in it that we breathe in with the air of the times."

In December 1950, when she was thirty-five, a sudden illness was diagnosed as the rheumatic disease of lupus, from which her father had died some years earlier. When her illness became increasingly incapacitating, Miss O'Connor returned to Georgia, to live the final four years of her life with her mother on a dairy farm, five miles outside Milledgeville. She devoted her remaining years to the ordeal of writing under a virtual sentence of death. Four weeks before she died of lupus, Flannery O'Connor wrote, "The wolf, I'm afraid, is inside tearing up the place. I've been in the hospital 50 days already this year." Of such courage are heroines made.

We must be grateful that no one confined Flannery O'Connor's imagination to the sterile acquisition of facts. Her work demonstrates that the human condition cannot be reduced to measurable parcels of fact that can be computed with precision. It demonstrates, too, the subtlety and complexity of the process by which gifted writers help us carry forward the preeminent task of liberal education: seeking understanding of the human condition.

Thomas Gradgrind regarded students, sitting at their desks, as "little vessels then and there arranged in order, ready to have imperial gallons of facts poured into them until they were full to the brim." The insistence in prominent sectors of American society that colleges stress the mastery of facts comes dangerously near to suggesting that liberal education is no more than an expensive investment in playing Trivial Pursuit. An academic emphasis on the acquisition of a static body of specific information is one of the surest routes to the closing of the American mind—to the closing of those very sources of mystery, insight, experience, and wisdom that illuminate the work of such writers, such heroines, as Flannery O'Connor.

Students are not "little vessels" ready to be filled with facts. They attend college not to be filled but to grow, not merely to memorize facts but to question assumptions, not just to absorb information but to awaken their critical capacities and to extend their creative sympathies. They attend college, in short, to participate in a commonwealth of liberal learning.

Originals and Copies

The opening of every new academic year inevitably makes me think of myself as a college student, aching with vague hopes and apprehensions, uncertain of what my calling in life might be, yearning for a great cause on which to focus my energies.

My own college years were during the Eisenhower administration—when television was still in black and white and the uniform of business was the gray flannel suit. A prominent book of the period was a collection of introspective essays by college students, entitled *The Unsilent Generation*—the self-portrait of a generation that was sharply criticized for its lack of idealism. A pervasive grayness hung over many of us—a fine silt of ennui that filtered into our dreams, dulled our sense of adventure, and dimmed our inchoate aspirations.

"Godless Communism," as it then was called, was the enemy, and after the protracted stalemate of Korea, it seemed likely that the cold war would go on forever—especially after Soviet tanks, in the fall of my senior year, crushed the brave hopes of the Hungarian freedom fighters. In defying the tyranny of the Soviet Union, those young people were the international heroes of my time, just as Lech Walesa, Václav Havel, and the courageous Chinese students of Tiananmen Square have been of recent years. But apart from those freedom fighters, we did not have any heroes of our own—and that, I think now, was part of our problem.

We thought of ourselves as living in a postheroic age, a time not of heroes but of antiheroes—diminished, Kafkaesque figures whose brooding alienation and misunderstood sensitivities expressed the shrinking limits of the human condition. We saw our world reflected in T. S. Eliot's *The Waste Land* and *The Hollow Men*. Our novelists were Albert Camus and J. D. Salinger; our filmmakers, Ingmar Bergman and François Truffaut; our playwrights, Samuel Beckett and Edward Albee; our philosophers, Reinhold Niebuhr and Jean-Paul Sartre; our cartoonists, Jules Feiffer and Walt Kelly; our best-selling manuals of cultural analysis, *The Organization Man* and *The Lonely Crowd*. Looming over us as a popular icon was the tormented figure of James Dean, dead in his twenties, forever inseparable from the existential role he played in the movie *Rebel Without A Cause*.

Now I wonder: what will today's college students look back on and identify, twenty or thirty years hence, as the formative influences on their own personal, intellectual, and social development? What influential books, what heroic figures, what great causes will they remember from their undergraduate years?

In his 1972 gathering of essays, *Sincerity and Authenticity*, Lionel Trilling quotes a plaintive query by the eighteenth-century poet Edward Young: "Born Originals," Young asks, "how comes it to pass that we die Copies?"

It is difficult for anyone, in an age of "Copies," to remain an "Original." Clearly it takes more than a formal curriculum to nourish within us an authentic sense of our being. At every stage of our development, in order to stimulate our moral and intellectual growth, we require the immediacy of human models. That is what Bernard Malamud must have meant when he wrote in *The Natural*, his haunting fable of a superachieving baseball star, "Without heroes, we're all plain people and don't know how far we can go."

The lives and works of three people have made them exemplars for me. All three happen to be Southerners: the first, a Mississippian, Eudora Welty; the second, an Alabamian, Hugo LaFayette Black; the third, a Georgian, Martin Luther King, Jr. In contemplating the lives and accomplishments of each of these three people—an imaginative writer, a passionate judge, and a transforming moral leader—one can see an "Original" character working out its own destiny. One is awed by their achievements. And one is prompted to search for the hidden roots of their creativity, the mysterious springs that fed their extraordinary capacity for lifelong growth and development, the inner resources that allowed them to transcend the confining limits of time and of place.

My first exemplar is Eudora Welty, whose greatness as a writer rests, in large measure, on the intensity of her experiences and observations, as both a Southerner and a woman. In work after amazing work—I think of the stories "Death of a Traveling Salesman," "Why I Live at the P.O.," "Livvie," and "A Worn Path," as well as such novels as *The Robber Bridegroom*, *Delta Wedding*, and *The Optimist's Daughter*—Welty brings into the mainstream of our awareness the overlooked, the undervalued, and the marginal. Her work is in the great tradition of Jane Austen, characterized by a wickedly playful wit, an exquisite ear for dialogue, a nuanced sensitivity to the small, everyday dramas of shy courtships and polite insults, and most of all by the universe of meaning that is revealed in the mundane fortunes of a single household.

Where did the strength of Welty's private life—her subtle powers of observation, compassion, and insight—come from? The answer must remain a mystery of the kind with which creative people often confound us. Welty herself has said only, "My imagination takes its strength and guides its direction from what I see and hear and learn and feel and remember of my living world. But I was to learn slowly that both these worlds, outer and inner, were different from what they seemed to me in the beginning."

With grace and energy, Eudora Welty has taught us that we have worlds to learn from a woman who never married, rarely traveled, and lived her entire life in the home in which she spent her childhood. Welty developed her private self even as she observed and engaged the public world. As she tellingly explains in the closing words of her literary autobiography, *One Writer's Beginnings*, "A sheltered life can be a daring life as well. For all serious daring starts from within."

My second exemplar is Hugo L. Black, who was born in a small wooden farmhouse in the Appalachian foothills of Clay County, Alabama, in 1886, the youngest child in a rural family of eight. He died in 1971 in Washington, D.C., where he had served eleven years as a United States senator and thirty-five years as a justice of the United States Supreme Court—one of the few people in our history to have held both of these high offices.

Hugo Black was a man of scant formal education, and little in his Alabama experience provided any basis for predicting the extraordinary intellectual growth that would characterize his career in the law. His public life illustrates more clearly than most the triumph of achieving an original and authentic being. Hugo Black's secret, revealed only after his confirmation, was that his path to Washington had led, briefly, through the dark swamp of the Ku Klux Klan. As a young trial lawyer in Birmingham, Hugo Black had joined the Klan in 1923 out of a tangle of motives, including the expedient desire to strengthen his hand before the Klan-dominated juries of the time. It is now clear that his judicial career was a sustained attempt to rectify this error.

In 1940, seventeen years after joining the Klan and three years after ascending to the Court, Justice Black wrote one of his most memorable opinions, *Chambers v. Florida*, overturning, as a violation of due process, the convictions of four impoverished black tenant farmers who, without benefit of counsel and after nine days and nights of relentless police questioning, had confessed to a murder. In a single, ringing sentence, Justice Black reproached and redeemed his past: "Under our constitutional system, courts stand against any winds that blow as havens of refuge for those who might otherwise suffer because they are helpless, weak, outnumbered, or because they are non-conforming victims of prejudice and public excitement."

In a length of service that spanned the presidencies of Roosevelt, Truman, Eisenhower, Kennedy, Johnson, and Nixon, Hugo Black pursued a personal course of reading and self-education probably unprecedented in the Court's history. From the *Annals* of Tacitus to the histories of Macaulay to the works of the Founders, Hugo Black immersed himself in history, economics, and philosophy, slowly forging a judicial philosophy that would profoundly influence the development of American constitutional law.

Judges with a distinctive, hard-earned constitutional philosophy are rare. By dint of a lifetime of study and reflection, Hugo Black became such a judge. A vigorously public man, he disciplined himself to cultivate his private self. As one of his law clerks recalled, Justice Black was always "on Mount Olympus, communing with the Constitution."

My third exemplar is Martin Luther King, Jr., a figure of towering intellectual influence and intriguing moral complexity. Much has been written on the genius of Dr. King's philosophy of nonviolence and the compelling power of his oratory. I want to focus on still another aspect of his life—his development as a moral thinker. Dr. King's biography is a tale of the steady maturation of his religious faith and his political and moral philosophy, to the elevating point of his perception, in *Letter from Birmingham Jail*, that "injustice anywhere is a threat to justice everywhere."

As the son of the pastor of one of the largest and most influential black congregations in the South, Martin Luther King, Jr., grew up with many cultural advantages. But these did not extend to the formal education available to him in the segregated schools of Atlanta in the 1930s and 1940s.

By the time that King was a senior at Morehouse College, he had developed a passionate desire to break free of his father's domination. Instead of attending a conservative Southern Baptist institution devoted exclusively to the preparation of black ministers for southern pulpits, he insisted on entering Crozer Theological Seminary in Chester, Pennsylvania. He was one of its first black students.

The intellectual atmosphere at Crozer was exactly what young Martin needed. As he read Kierkegaard and Niebuhr, as he studied the classical Greek philosophers and the early Church Fathers, as he matched wits with his freethinking professors (some of whom were agnostics), King began to develop a philosophical position of his own, and he began to think of a career as a professor of theology. Instead of returning to the South to preach, King entered Boston University, where he wrote a dissertation on the theology of Paul Tillich and earned his Ph.D.

Facing the need to support his growing family while writing his dissertation, King decided to gain some experience as a pastor after all. At twenty-six years of age, he competed for and won the prestigious pulpit of the Dexter Avenue Baptist Church in Montgomery in 1954, just two weeks before *Brown v. Board of Education* was decided, and only a few months before Rosa Parks refused to give up, for a white passenger, her seat on a Montgomery bus.

The senior ministers in the black community of Montgomery immediately recognized King's gifts as a leader. They lost no time in inviting their young colleague to organize and direct the Montgomery bus boycott. From 1955 onward, King channeled his imposing intellectual abilities into the action for social and political reform that became his life's work. And yet, in the very years in which his public life must have seemed all-consuming, Martin Luther King, Jr., found the moral and intellectual reserves to continue to cultivate a private self of philosophic contemplation.

When Dr. King spoke of his struggle to an all-male, preponderantly white audience at Dartmouth College on May 23, 1962, he made a prophetic claim for his movement. "Our victory shall be a double victory," he said, "we shall win our opponents in the process." King was only thirty-three years old then, with not quite six years more to live.

By the time that Dr. King was assassinated in April 1968, he had broadened his witness on behalf of blacks to include the poor and all oppressed minorities; he had extended his political agenda to take in economic as well as racial issues; he had expanded his moral vision to embrace the cause of peace as well as that of social justice.

And so I return to Edward Young's question: "Born Originals, how comes it to pass that we die Copies?" The three exemplars from my own development were born "Originals," as each of us was. But how comes it to pass that, in them, the erosive pressures of daily life, the trivializing tendencies toward social and intellectual conformity, did not succeed in reducing them to "Copies"? How comes it to pass that, on the contrary, these pressures and tendencies sharpened their distinctive characters and called forth their unique contributions to our culture?

By their unusual capacities to know who they truly were, by their remarkable abilities to grow in understanding and expression, and by their focused commitment to achieve their destinies, Eudora Welty and Hugo Black and Martin Luther King, Jr., each lived the life of an "Original." They were not unconventional or odd—merely authentically themselves. In providing models of how an heroic life can be led, they teach us the importance of achieving a grip on our identity and a sense of our own calling.

Those Who Are Truly Great

The meditative Eastern trader, Stein, says in Joseph Conrad's novel *Lord Jim*, "In general, adapting the words of your great poet: That is the question. . . . How to be!"

In confronting that momentous question—a question often avoided because its weight makes us uncomfortable—we can take valuable guidance from the lives and accomplishments of people who inspire us—people who, in the words of the English poet Stephen Spender, are "truly great . . . those who in their lives fought for life, / Who wore at their hearts the fire's centre."

People who are truly great are important to us because their lives embody abundance and possibility. They are exemplars of the best that individuals can seek and achieve. They are emblems of moral substance, of personal resourcefulness, and of intellectual growth. They are talismans for inspiration and rejuvenation at those hollow moments when we feel depressed and defeated, captured by life's pettiness, wearied by the dreaded fear that, in the end, life comes to naught.

Now I wonder: for today's college students, who will one day be those heroes in their lives who "wore at their hearts the fire's centre"?

I often speak to students about a man whose achievements have made him an exemplar in my life, George F. Kennan. At a time of fundamental change in the former Soviet Union, George Kennan's accomplishments as a Russian historian and a principal architect of postwar American foreign policy are especially noteworthy.

George Kennan was born in Milwaukee in 1904. Perhaps it is reassuring to learn that a man who would become such a prominent American intellectual entered Princeton poorly prepared academically (he described himself later as "the last student admitted") and that his academic performance there was undistinguished. Alienated by what he considered Princeton's environment of social snobbery, Kennan felt himself an outsider, socially and intellectually. Many years later, writing of his college experience, Kennan recalled, "Yet cruel as it was, there was something useful in the experience. It finally dawned on me . . . that to be fair to oneself one had to make one's own standards, one could not just accept those of other

155

people; there was always the possibility that those others, in the very rejection of us, had been wrong." In that early insight, one sees evidence of Kennan's lifelong tendency to a sturdy independence of mind and a skeptical wariness of the Establishment.

Kennan graduated from Princeton "not really awakened" and not especially curious intellectually. The only thing of which he was certain was that he did not want to return to Milwaukee. Not knowing what else to do, he took the Foreign Service examination—and passed. He hoped that the Foreign Service would protect him from falling into an occupational rut.

The State Department assigned Kennan overseas immediately, posting him, first, to a number of European cities—including Geneva, Hamburg, Tallinn, and Riga—that served as "listening posts" around the Soviet Union; and, next, to the University of Berlin, so that he might immerse himself in Russian language, history, and culture. When the United States recognized the Soviet government in 1933, Kennan, not yet thirty, accompanied America's first ambassador to Moscow.

Four years later, on returning to the United States after nearly a decade abroad, Kennan felt "that peculiar loneliness of the returned exile," estranged from the uncongenial country that the United States had become, longing, as he said, for "everything America had once been; and [with] a decided reluctance to identify myself with what it seemed to be becoming." Then, as later, Kennan felt himself to be a "guest in one's time and not a member of its household."

During World War II Kennan served in the American embassies in Lisbon and Moscow, before returning to the United States as director of the State Department's Policy Planning Staff. From 1946 to 1950, as one of the government's acknowledged experts on Soviet affairs, Kennan engaged in the day-to-day formulation of foreign policy at the most senior levels of the State Department.

His growing influence on American diplomacy was significantly enhanced with the publication, in July 1947, of his famous "Mr. X article" in *Foreign Affairs*. The essay, published under the pseudonym X, expressed reservations about resting American foreign policy on the hope of building trust with the Soviet Union. Arguing that conciliation and appeasement of the Soviet Union would not work because of Russia's instinctive sense of insecurity and its commitment to world domination, he called for a policy of containment based, as he wrote in a famous phrase, on "the adroit and vigilant application of counterforce at a series of constantly shifting geographical and political points."

Kennan's proposal for a policy of containment became the underpinning of the Truman Doctrine, the Marshall Plan, the North Atlantic

Treaty Organization, and the Berlin Airlift. Few career diplomats have attained such influence. For the next forty years, Kennan's conception of containment remained a firm, if controversial, cornerstone of American foreign policy.

Yet Kennan—for all the satisfaction he might have taken from such influence—was repelled by the virulence of the anti-Communist rhetoric of the cold war decades and by the headlong acceleration of the nuclear arms race. As he often stated publicly, he preferred to emphasize the importance of following a rational, disciplined foreign policy based on a recognition of the balance of power and a respect for the zones of vital interest of the contending superpowers.

As could be expected, Kennan's criticisms of American foreign policy were not well received in the State Department. Never, perhaps, was Kennan more acutely aware that he was both an insider to the making of foreign policy and an outsider to the foreign policy establishment than on the day in 1953 when Secretary of State John Foster Dulles informed him that, after twenty-seven years, his career in the Foreign Service was at an end. In criticizing the policies of his superiors, Kennan had ignored the pressure of conformity.

Having thus been forced to retire at an early age, Kennan embraced scholarship as his principal vocation. He joined the Institute for Advanced Study at Princeton, where he wrote more than twenty books, including a history of Soviet-American relations during World War I and his *Memoirs*, each of which earned him a Pulitzer Prize.

During the later decades of his life, Kennan was deeply disturbed by "the obvious deterioration in the quality both of American life itself and of the natural environment in which it had its being, under the impact of a headlong overpopulation, industrialization, commercialization and urbanization of society." Even the exercise of foreign affairs he increasingly found to be, as he wrote, "an empty one; for what use was there, I had to ask, in attempting to protect in its relations to others a society that was clearly failing in its relation to itself?" He scorned the war in Vietnam as a monumental error giving further evidence of America's moral decadence and intellectual incompetence. And he disapproved of what he regarded as the self-indulgent behavior and values of the student Left during the turbulent years of the 1960s.

Burdened by a growing feeling of intellectual loneliness, Kennan sought "in the interpretation of history a usefulness I could not find in the interpretation of my own time." Adopting the outsider status of a scholar, he conscientiously distanced himself from the immediacy of events precisely so that he could better contribute to understanding them.

In accepting the Grenville Clark Award at Dartmouth College in

1981, Kennan expressed a forceful criticism of the Soviet Union, lest he be misunderstood as a Soviet apologist, and then went on to say:

> I find the view of the Soviet Union that prevails today in our governmental and journalistic establishments so extreme, so subjective, so far removed from what any sober scrutiny of external reality would reveal, that it is not only ineffective but dangerous as a guide to political action. This endless series of distortions and oversimplifications; this systematic dehumanization of the leadership of another great country; this routine exaggeration of Moscow's military capabilities and of the supposed iniquity of its intentions; this daily misrepresentation of the nature and the attitudes of another great people—and a long-suffering people at that, sorely tried by the vicissitudes of this past century; this ignoring of their pride, their hopes—yes, even of their illusions (for they have their illusions, just as we have ours; and illusions, too, deserve respect); this reckless application of the double standard to the judgment of Soviet conduct and our own; this failure to recognize the communality of many of their problems and ours as we both move inexorably into the modern technological age; and this corresponding tendency to view all aspects of the relationship in terms of a supposed total and irreconcilable conflict of concerns and aims: these, believe me, are not the marks of the maturity and realism one expects of the diplomacy of a great power; they are the marks of an intellectual primitivism and naivety unpardonable in a great government.

In his *Memoirs*, Kennan described himself as uncomfortable with his contemporaries and his nation, partial to the temper of the eighteenth century, and envious of the life of a cultivated European. He believed that American politics had become mundane and trivial and that civilized society had entered a spiral of decline. To some, his adherence to older, more formal standards of political conduct and personal behavior appeared to be elitist and snobbish; perhaps in these respects he gravitated toward the near occasion of sin. But his brooding discomfort with his time and place as well as his significant frustration at failing to effect change in American foreign policy must have caused him to ponder Nathaniel Hawthorne's somber view that "a hero cannot be a hero unless in an heroic world."

Kennan considered the spontaneous tribute paid him by Mikhail Gorbachev, at a reception at the Soviet embassy during Gorbachev's historic visit to Washington in 1987, to be the crowning closure to his life's work. Although he had never met Gorbachev before, Kennan wrote that Gorbachev "amazed me by throwing out his arms and treating me to what has now become the standard statesman's embrace. Then, still holding on to my elbows, he looked me seriously in the eye and said: 'Mr. Kennan. We in our country believe that a man may be the friend of another country and remain, at the same time, a loyal and devoted citizen of his own; and that is the way we view you.'"

In Kennan's reaction to Gorbachev's tribute one senses the personal anguish he must have felt, caught as he was in the fateful tension of being both an insider and an outsider to the making of American foreign policy: "I reflected that if you cannot have this sort of recognition from your own government to ring down your involvement in such a relationship, it is nice to have it at least from the one-time adversary."

In the end, George Kennan's inestimable effectiveness and influence stemmed from his daunting integrity, his refusal to trim his views to fit the fashion of the moment, and his willingness to relinquish the heady satisfactions of power that were his as an insider in order to preserve his moral authority as an outsider.

We live today in a society of self-promotion and networking, a culture obsessed with who is in and who is out, who is hot and who is not, a country mesmerized by the meretricious tinsel of fame. If our society truly cares about excellence, we must celebrate those heroes and heroines who achieve the disciplined dignity of intellectual independence. The life of George F. Kennan provides an elevating example of such heroic achievement.

Ordinary Backgrounds, Extraordinary Men

Ralph J. Bunche and Harry S. Truman were two very different individuals who had much in common. They both came from ordinary backgrounds but developed into extraordinary persons of extraordinary achievement.

There was little indication in the outward circumstances of their early lives that either would achieve greatness. Yet each helped to shape the postwar world and guide the United States and the United Nations into an era of vast and unprecedented responsibilities. Ralph Bunche and Harry Truman each had an unwavering sense of who he was and a rare ability to be guided by that knowledge, even in the face of such obstacles as early personal failure, tight economic circumstances, and racial discrimination.

Ralph Bunche was one of this nation's most significant figures during the middle decades of the twentieth century: an international civil servant of great distinction and the recipient of the Nobel Prize for Peace. Yet his reputation has been in eclipse in recent years, his achievements in danger of being less appreciated by history than they ought to be.

He was born in Detroit in 1903, the son of an itinerant barber, and reared in Albuquerque and Los Angeles. Years later, Bunche would write of his family, "We bowed to no one, we worked hard and never felt any shame about having little money." Bunche was graduated from the University of California, Los Angeles, in 1927, as valedictorian of his class. From that auspicious intellectual beginning, he followed the example of his boyhood hero, W. E. B. Du Bois, and went to Harvard to pursue both his master's and his Ph.D. degrees. There he demonstrated the remarkable capacity for concentration and work that characterized his entire life.

Bunche began his career as a professor of political science at Howard University, but he was never happy there. He abhorred the racial segregation that then existed in Washington. He chafed under what he regarded as Howard's parochial nature and was especially frustrated by the university's failure to acknowledge that the interests of African-Americans—Bunche himself always used the word *Negro*—were linked to those of oppressed peoples around the world. To Ralph Bunche, the rise of fascism in Europe, for example, was a clear threat to the security and status of African-Americans.

Therefore, when opportunities presented themselves to get away from Howard and from Washington, Bunche seized them. In 1939, Gunnar Myrdal, the Swedish social economist, was enlisted by the Carnegie Corporation of New York to direct "a comprehensive study of the Negro in the United States, to be undertaken in a wholly objective and dispassionate way as a social phenomenon."

Myrdal engaged Bunche as one of his top staff members, and for several traumatic months, they traveled together throughout the South, observing firsthand the deplorable conditions in which the American Negro was forced to live. Eventually, Bunche wrote four supporting monographs for Myrdal, the most important of which was sixteen hundred pages long. Myrdal's study, published in 1944 as *An American Dilemma*, was acclaimed as a seminal work. Indeed, it played an influential role, a decade later, in the Supreme Court's decision in *Brown v. Board of Education* (1954), which held segregation in public schools unconstitutional.

From this triumph of scholarship came opportunities for Bunche to move into the field of diplomacy. Within several years, his stature enabled him to play a major role in the San Francisco conference that established the United Nations. In the process, he came to appreciate that his talents would find their most valuable use in international service.

From 1946, when he served as a member of the United States delegation to the first session of the United Nations General Assembly, until his death in 1971, Dr. Bunche's career as undersecretary of the United Nations was devoted to peacemaking. He undertook diplomatic efforts around the world, from Palestine to the Suez, from Yemen to the Congo, from Cyprus to Kashmir, and finally in Vietnam. In 1950 he was awarded the Nobel Prize for Peace for his work in negotiating an armistice agreement between Israel and its Arab adversaries.

In his recent biography, *Ralph Bunche—An American Life*, Brian Urquhart describes the sources of Bunche's professional success: "His stamina, his charm, his capacity for inspiring personal confidence and respect, his unwavering honesty, his ability to keep things going in critical situations, his understanding of the preoccupations and fears of the negotiators, his unique knowledge of the situation on the ground, and his brilliance, originality and speed in drafting, all combined to make an extraordinary impression on those he dealt with."

Ralph Bunche died in 1971, before most of today's undergraduates were born. Yet his achievements as a public servant and a person of character shaped the world they inherit.

Harry S. Truman was an ordinary man who became an extraordinary president. Born in 1884 and raised in Independence, Missouri, he never departed from the simple values of his Midwestern, agrarian youth or of the quieter century into which he was born. Those values included honesty and hard work, fair play and personal integrity. His credo, as David McCullough wrote in his magnificent biography, *Truman*, was simple: "Say what you mean, mean what you say. . . . Keep your word. Never get too big for your britches. Never forget a friend."

Harry Truman did not attend college. He was a self-educated man—throughout his lifetime a voracious reader, of history especially, from Plutarch to Macaulay. His daughter, Margaret, could not recall a time when her father, sitting quietly at home, did not have a book in his hand.

After completing high school, Truman worked successively as a bank clerk, a land and mining speculator, and a farmer. Although he could have avoided service in World War I on several counts, including poor eyesight, he enlisted as a captain of a field-artillery battery and saw fierce and bloody action in France. From that traumatic experience, he discovered that he had a gift for leadership.

After the war, Truman opened a men's clothing store in Kansas City. Within three years, the business failed, saddling him with debts that he insisted on paying off in full, even though it took him nearly twenty years to do so. In conscientiously meeting his financial obligations to his creditors, rather than wiping out their claims by filing for bankruptcy, Truman demonstrated the depth of his moral character, even as he would on so many later occasions.

It was only at the age of thirty-eight that he entered politics—some have suggested out of desperation—and won election to the Jackson County Court; the future president of the United States became, in essence, a county commissioner. He performed his responsibilities with an efficiency and probity quite uncharacteristic of the Democratic Party machine in Kansas City, which had sponsored his political career.

Truman was elected to the United States Senate in 1934 and reelected in 1940. His work as chairman of a special Senate committee investigating corruption and inefficiency in World War II military procurement was widely praised, and in 1944 he was chosen as Franklin Delano Roosevelt's vice presidential running mate. When Roosevelt died, on April 12, 1945, only eighty-two days after he had been sworn in for his fourth term, Harry S. Truman became president of the United States.

Succeeding Roosevelt was a daunting experience. It felt, Truman said, "like the moon, the stars, and all the planets had fallen on me." The challenges that confronted him were Herculean, especially that of dealing with the Soviet Union and with the onset of the cold war. Truman was not even told about the Manhattan Project until he had been president for twelve days; shortly thereafter, he had to make the decision of whether to use the atomic bomb against Japan.

Truman's achievements as president were formidable. In foreign affairs, he devised the doctrine of containment toward the Soviet Union. He formulated the Truman Doctrine, which committed the United States to assist anti-Communist forces in Greece and Turkey; and, after an invasion by North Korean forces, he sent American forces into battle in South Korea. He implemented the Marshall Plan for rebuilding Western Europe, ordered the Berlin Airlift, and created the North American Treaty Organization. He recognized the State of Israel—making the United States the first nation to do so—and firmly committed the United States to support of the newly born United Nations.

On the domestic front, Truman's Fair Deal sought to continue the work of Roosevelt's New Deal. Although his origins were in a border state where Jim Crow still prevailed and Confederate nostalgia lingered, Truman knew from historical reflection and humane instinct that racial discrimination was wrong. He desegregated the armed forces and the civil service by executive order, and, at great cost to his political fortunes, he advocated the nation's first meaningful civil rights program, seeking legal protection against lynching, poll taxes, and employment discrimination.

As Justice Thurgood Marshall said many years later in praising President Truman's bravery and character, Truman "risked losing his chance at his own term as president" by confronting the power of Southern segregationist senators. "I tell you again," Justice Marshall said, "that when all the history books are written, Truman is going to come out on top."

Through most of his nearly eight years in office, Truman was an unpopular president. Some believed that his foreign policy helped to initiate the cold war and that his loyalty program encouraged the witch-hunts of the McCarthy era. Others regarded him as incompetent, unsophisticated, undignified. Walter Lippmann, perhaps the leading journalist of the day, considered Truman a national embarrassment, and Washington wits observed, "To err is Truman."

Despite constant criticism, Truman never lost his sturdy optimism, his jaunty self-confidence, or his unshakable conviction that his principles were right. He began the 1948 presidential campaign as a distinct underdog, but his combative style and unvarnished rhetoric attracted large crowds, which often shouted, "Give 'em hell, Harry." In the end, Truman achieved the most stunning political upset in American history. His victory over Thomas E. Dewey was commemorated by the famous photograph of a triumphant Truman holding up an early edition of the Chicago *Tribune* that carried the headline "Dewey Defeats Truman." Virtually everyone was surprised except, apparently, Truman himself, who had gone to bed before the results were in.

Harry S. Truman—nearsighted artillery officer, failed haberdasher, machine politician—rose to the challenge of the most powerful office on earth. He accepted fully the responsibility proclaimed by the slogan he kept on his desk: The Buck Stops Here. As Mary McGrory wrote after his death, Harry Truman "proved that the ordinary American is capable of grandeur." It was Winston Churchill who said to Truman, toward the end of his presidency, "The last time you and I sat across the conference table was at Potsdam, Mr. President. I must confess, sir, I held you in very low regard then. I loathed your taking the place of Franklin Roosevelt. I misjudged you badly. Since that time, you more than any other man, have saved Western civilization."

The reasons that Truman was able to rise to the challenge of the presidency derive, surely, from his character. Throughout his life Truman remained open to experience, finding opportunities in crises and converting adversity into a crucible of personal growth. Even amidst the pressures and cynicism of politics, Truman retained the bedrock values of his youth when, as he later said, "right was right and wrong was wrong, and you didn't have to *talk* about it."

What lessons do the lives of Ralph J. Bunche and Harry S. Truman teach today's undergraduates? They teach that a person who engages in a lifelong pursuit of education, beyond the school and college years, can continue to grow in understanding and moral stature. By reading and reflecting throughout their lives, Bunche and Truman gained a sympathetic understanding of history and human nature. More than that, they remained intellectually vital and prepared themselves for the momentous opportunities that history eventually would place before them.

Essayists and Solitude

Much of our lives will be spent in solitary activities—thinking, reading, writing, studying, or waiting. Nevertheless, as effective as many colleges may be at nurturing admirable qualities, they are not as good as they ought to be at preparing individuals to confront the quiet and the solitude—the resounding silence—that the human condition inevitably presents and that many realms of human satisfaction require.

It is worth remembering that not long ago, one day of every week was sealed in relative silence and insulated against the clanging urgency of work. Then, the Sabbath was dedicated to prayer, worship, reading, and thinking. Imagine how different one's life would be today if each Saturday or Sunday were reserved solely for contemplative endeavors! It is appropriate, therefore, that we consider the importance of silence and of solitude in providing a respite from the chatter of the daily world, in nurturing the private self, and in creating a healthy and productive thoughtfulness.

Everywhere we look, the world urges us to avoid the pleasures of silence—to turn on the radio or the television, to make a phone call, to see a movie, to leap to where the action is—above all, to be active. Many people, I fear, regard contemplative endeavors, like reading and writing, as too low-tech, too labor-intensive, too solitary, too quiet to be personally satisfying. We often act as if silence and solitude are conditions to be avoided at all costs—out of a fear, perhaps, that left alone with our thoughts and feelings, we may discover that we do not have any, or that we do not make very good company for ourselves, or, worst of all, that we utterly lack a private self.

Unfortunately, it is those persons who enter a room like a marching band who commandeer our immediate attention. The voices of quieter, more thoughtful people—of thinkers and writers, of philosophers and dreamers—frequently get overwhelmed by the din. Some of those are the quiet voices of the printed page, and here I am thinking especially of essayists.

The essayist's craft is a function not only of creativity but also of an exceptional thoughtfulness and a rare ability to observe, describe, and analyze. Essayists lead us to think about things that we might otherwise not have thought about—ideas remote from our usual considerations, distant from the beaten track of our minds—informing profoundly what we see and do and think. More than many other writers, essayists explore what Socrates called "the examined life"—examined in the double sense of being keenly observed and deeply considered. That is the great appeal and power both of the classic essayists—Montaigne, Bacon, Addison, Steele, Emerson—and of the most engaging essayists of our own time—E. B. White, James Thurber, Virginia Woolf, James Baldwin, V. S. Pritchett.

I should like to consider two essayists—one British, one American—whose works reward thoughtful and quiet consideration. They are George Orwell and Edmund Wilson.

For many people the name George Orwell is synonymous with his two most famous books, which, although nominally novels, are in their didactic content closely akin to essays. The first, *Animal Farm*, is a parable, a brilliant satire on the Russian Revolution, published in 1945, after four publishers (including T. S. Eliot at Faber and Faber) had rejected it on the ground that it attacked a wartime ally. In it, Orwell set out his ironic formulation of the governing commandment of totalitarian revolution: "All Animals Are Equal. But Some Animals Are More Equal than Others."

The second, *Nineteen Eighty-Four* (1949), is one of the most important books of this century—a chilling cautionary tale of a totalitarian society in which history, language, and truth itself are manipulated to serve the police state. In the world of Orwell's *Nineteen Eighty-Four*, there is no science, for truth is only that false image of reality that the state has fashioned for its own uses. There is no literature, for language has been "cut to the bone" to remove nuance and to narrow the range of thought. There is not even any history, for the records of the past have been altered beyond recovery or recognition in order to serve the ends of the state. All that there is, finally, is Orwell's vision of "a boot stamping on a human face—for ever." Orwellian coinages like Big Brother, Doublethink, Newspeak, and Unperson have become clichés, precisely because they define phenomena all too familiar in the world around us.

Although Orwell's fame as a novelist is great, in the end his reputation may come to rest equally on his work as an essayist. Orwell's essays are numerous, their subjects diverse: autobiography, culture, literary criticism, sociology, and politics. They established him, in many ways, as the conscience of his time. In many of his essays, Orwell writes of his beloved England, and he does so with characteristic bifocal vision, noting its humane gentleness, as well as its harsh imperialism and class privilege.

In his autobiographical essay "Shooting an Elephant," Orwell recounts his experiences as a British police officer in Burma, when "I was hated by large numbers of people—the only time in my life that I have been important enough for this to happen to me." He was compelled by the will of the defenseless Burmese to shoot a rogue elephant that had destroyed property and killed a man. As he confronted their expectation that he restore order, Orwell came to see that his own judgment of how to handle the situation counted for naught and that, ironically, "when the white man turns tyrant it is his own freedom that he destroys."

Orwell's great legacy is his uncompromising commitment to intellectual integrity. He vigorously asserted his independence of mind, often in a newspaper column with the telling title, "As I Please." He was a dedicated Socialist as well as a fervent anti-Communist, but he had the lonely courage to despise, in one of his recurring themes, all the "smelly little orthodoxies" that endangered freedom of thought. He was, in his own words, a "Tory anarchist."

Orwell could not be satisfied with complacent or expedient answers to complex questions. Thus, he was a militant leftist who attacked the Left for its willingness to ignore facts, as he felt it had done by turning a forgiving eye toward Stalinist Communism, and for its disposition to manipulate truth, as he felt it had done in glorifying war in support of the struggle in Spain against Francisco Franco.

In his most influential essay, "Politics and the English Language," Orwell emphasizes the necessity of clarity of expression to political and moral well-being. Style is substance, Orwell insists, and prose that is slack, clichéd, and hackneyed will produce thinking that is confused, evasive, and dishonest.

For all his intellectual and moral sternness, Orwell nonetheless cared deeply for people, and he keenly understood the complexities of right and wrong. "The essence of being human," he wrote in his essay "Reflections on Gandhi," "is that one does not seek perfection, that one *is* sometimes willing to commit sins for the sake of loyalty, that one does not push asceticism to the point where it makes friendly intercourse impossible, and that one is prepared in the end to be defeated and broken up by life, which is the inevitable price of fastening one's love upon other human individuals."

Edmund Wilson was born in 1895. After being graduated in 1916 from Princeton, where he began a lifelong friendship with F. Scott Fitzgerald, Wilson served in World War I with the American Expeditionary Force in France before becoming a newspaper reporter. He later wrote literary and cultural criticism for *Vanity Fair*, the *New Republic*, and the *New Yorker*. Only a few years out of Princeton, Wilson already seemed, as Lionel Trilling recalled, "in his own person, and young as he was, to propose and to realize the idea of the literary life."

A prolific author, Wilson published more than thirty books. He regarded the solitary work of the writer as an expression of character. In 1937, he wrote to the poet Louise Bogan, urging her to respond to a nervous collapse by applying herself to her poetry. "We have to take life—society and human relations—more or less as we find them," Wilson declared. "The only thing that we can really make is our work. And deliberate work of the mind, imagination, and hand, done, as Nietzsche said, 'notwithstanding,' in the long run remakes the world."

Three of Wilson's most influential books are collections of essays. *Axel's Castle*, published in 1931, established Wilson's reputation as a literary critic. It was a pioneering study that celebrated six modern masters—Yeats, Valéry, Eliot, Proust, Joyce, and Stein—and demonstrated that, in their energy and innovativeness, "they belong to a common school," which he termed Symbolism. Wilson especially championed Joyce's *Ulysses* and *Finnegans Wake* and the early works of T. S. Eliot, which, he asserted, "break down the walls of the present and wake us to the hope and exaltation of the untried, unsuspected possibilities of human thought and art." Even now, *Axel's Castle* remains an invaluable guide to the intellectual and artistic worlds of those writers who shaped so decisively the literary sensibilities of the twentieth century.

In *To the Finland Station*, a study of nineteenth-century revolutionaries, published in 1940, Wilson blended—as his works often did—biography, history, and criticism, to examine the makers of the Russian Revolution, most particularly Marx, Lenin, and Trotsky. Although Wilson finds no merit in the Marxist dialectic, he admires the sacrifice and dedication of those who sought to bring the Socialist ideal to Russia. The book, often described as the classic account of the heroic tradition of Socialism, contains one of literature's most compelling portraits of Karl Marx. In that essay, Wilson also explores his own lifelong theme of the relationship between neurosis and trauma on the one hand, creative power and action on the other.

Patriotic Gore, published in 1962, is a comprehensive study of the consciousness of Civil War America, based on the diaries, letters, memoirs, speeches, and other accounts of the men and women who bore the battle and endured the war. Wilson's essays reinterpreted many of the major figures of the period, including not only Lincoln, Grant, Sherman, and Lee but also Frederick Law Olmsted, Kate Chopin, Ambrose Bierce, Harriet Beecher Stowe, and Mary Chesnut. In many respects, the book is an American version of Plutarch's *Lives*.

Perhaps the finest of the portraits in *Patriotic Gore* is that of Oliver Wendell Holmes, Jr., three times wounded in action, yet still prepared to believe, as he would later say, that "it is required of a man that he should share the passion and action of his time at peril of being judged not to have lived." In assessing Holmes's achievements as a justice of the United States Supreme Court, Wilson asks: "How was it that he managed to survive, to function as a first-rate intellect, to escape the democratic erosion?" The answer to this question (in which Wilson so clearly identifies with Holmes) lies, he says, in the fact that Holmes "never dissociates himself from the great world of thought and art, and that all his decisions are written with awareness of both their wider implications and the importance of their literary form."

As he grew older, Edmund Wilson increasingly became an outsider in his own country. His remoteness stemmed from both a disaffection with the nation's cultural goals, particularly its rampant acquisitiveness, and an abhorrence of a proliferating defense budget. For ten years he refused to pay his income tax—a Thoreauvian tactic that cost him dearly in his ultimate accounting with the government. However, if Wilson's distance from the center of American life reinforced a certain crabbedness in his temperament, causing some to fear that he was lapsing into the misanthropy of H. L. Mencken, it also enabled him in his later years to see and report on the nation's social and political life with a wry astringency. For example, he wrote, "Robert Lowell has done something very extraordinary; he has made poetry out of modern Boston."

As the range of his books indicates—he also wrote on the Dead Sea Scrolls, Canadian and Russian literature, and Native American culture, in addition to publishing novels and plays—Wilson was a true man of letters. His incisive mind and aggressive curiosity, his intellectual energy and imagination, his courage to be idiosyncratic, his interest in language and character, and his resistance to popular fads enabled him to continue to learn throughout his life and to say so much of import until its very end. In 1963, President Lyndon B. Johnson awarded Wilson the Presidential Medal of Freedom. The citation read, "Critic and historian, he has converted criticism itself into a creative act, while setting for the Nation a stern and uncompromising standard of independent judgment."

It is no coincidence that both George Orwell and Edmund Wilson were models of an uncompromising commitment to excellence, to intellectual integrity, and to political independence. They were not confined within the prosaic bounds of conventional thought. Each was simultaneously engaged with his material and removed from it. In making unflinchingly honest appraisals of his subjects, each let sympathy and judgment fall where they might, pursuing truth to conclusions that often were unconventional or politically incorrect. We would be well served to reflect on the kind of intellectual integrity and strength of character that they possessed.

Index

Abortion, 12, 139, 143
Accent, 146
Access to education, 64
Acheson, Dean, 11, 122
Achievement of T. S. Eliot, The (Matthiessen), 13–14
Acton, Lord, 16
Adams, Henry, 3, 56
Adams, John, 36, 85
Addison, Joseph, 168
Address Unknown (Taylor), 34–35
Administration, academic, 19, 20, 23, 49
Admissions, 24, 27, 65, 66, 123, 140
Advancement of Learning, The (Bacon), 71
Advocate, The Harvard, 36
Affirmative action, 66
Affluent Society, The (Galbraith), 13
Agee, James, 17, 39
Age of Enlightenment, 85
Age of Reform, The (Hofstadter), 13
Albee, Edward, 149
Allegory, 29, 146
All the King's Men (Warren), 36
Altruism, 2, 3
Always the Young Strangers (Sandburg), 99, 108
Ambition, 3, 10, 11, 22, 23, 29, 63, 70, 106
"America Is Promises" (MacLeish), 119
American Dilemma, An (Myrdal), 45, 133, 134, 162
American Revolution, 83, 85

American Scholar, 37
"American Scholar, The" (Emerson), 102
Ammons, A. R., 27
Anatomy of Criticism (Frye), 13
Anderson, Sherwood, 10
Animal Farm (Orwell), 168
Annals (Tacitus), 152
Anti-Semitism, 12, 35, 113, 121
Apley, George, 78
Aquinas, St. Thomas, 28, 72
Arendt, Hannah, 22
Areopagitica (Milton), 45
Aristotle, 22, 87
Arrowsmith (Lewis), 34
Arts, 1, 22, 23, 26, 27, 28, 32, 63, 86, 87, 101, 105, 112, 170, 171; creative, 23, 24, 123; liberal, 24, 25, 71, 77–80, 86, 114, 115, 148; performing, 23, 24
"As I Please" (Orwell), 169
"Asphodel, That Greeny Flower" (Williams), 25
Athletics, 24, 63, 65, 66
Auden, W. H., 14, 44, 93, 97, 100
Austen, Jane, 4, 22, 73, 150
Autobiography, 38, 80, 99, 108, 151, 168, 169
Axel's Castle (Wilson), 170

Babbitt (Lewis), 34
Bacon, Francis, 16, 71, 72, 75, 79, 168
Baker, Carlos H., 21
Baker v. Carr, 16
Baldwin, James, 168
Bate, Walter Jackson, 14, 29, 45

Bates College, 9
Beadle, George W., 21
Beadle, Muriel, 21
Beauvoir, Simone de, 146
Beckett, Samuel, 14, 149
Beecher, Lyman, 83–84
Bel Geddes, Barbara, 12
Bellow, Saul, 27, 108
Benavente, Jacinto, 44
Bennett, William J., 56, 57, 82
Bergman, Ingmar, 149
Bergson, Henri, 127
Berlin, Sir Isaiah, 13
Berlin airlift, 157, 164
Berlin Wall, 27
Best and the Brightest, The (Halber-
   stam), 45
Bible, 43, 85, 122
Bickel, Alexander M., 13, 15, 16, 58,
   106–7, 108
Bierce, Ambrose, 170
Big Ten. See University
Bill of Rights, 126, 142
Bill of Rights, The (Hand), 58
Billy Budd (Melville), 23
Biography, 14, 17, 29, 31, 36, 45, 129,
   132, 152, 162, 163, 170
Black, Charles L., Jr., 15, 133
Black, Hugo Lafayette, 3, 126, 138,
   150, 151–52, 153
Blackmun, Harry A., 66
Blackstone, William, 85
Blake, William, 79
Bloom, Allan, 56, 57
Bloom, Claire, 28
Bogan, Louise, 170
Book-of-the-Month Club, 36
Books, 12, 13, 14, 16, 21, 28, 29, 43,
   44, 45, 46, 47, 69, 71, 82, 100, 106,
   146, 149, 150, 157, 163, 164, 168,
   170, 171; collecting, 31–41, 43; list
   (see "Great books;" Reading list);
   stores, 33, 34, 40
Boorstin, Daniel, 83, 134
Boston Globe, 10
Boston University, 152

Boswell, James, 31
Bowen, Catherine Drinker, 36
Boyle, T. Coraghessan, 24
Brandeis, Louis Dembitz, 12, 32, 49,
   119, 120–23, 124, 127, 130
Brennan, William J., Jr., 136, 138, 139,
   140
Bridges, Robert, 14
Bridgman, Percy, 78
Brighton Rock (Greene), 40
Brodsky, Joseph, 28
Brown v. Board of Education, 16, 45,
   61, 62, 96, 107, 130, 133, 134, 137,
   138, 139, 153, 162
Bryant, William Cullen, 85
Bunche, Ralph J., 3, 161–62, 165
Bureaucracy, 18, 20, 70, 112
Burger, Warren E., 138
Burke, Edmund, 23, 86, 96, 107, 114
Burt, Robert A., 120, 122, 123, 126
Bush, Douglas, 14, 36–37
Butler, Samuel, 80
Buttrick, George A., 14
By Love Possessed (Cozzens), 17

Cabell, James Branch, 10
Cahan, Abraham, 10, 13
Cakes and Ale (Maugham), 34
Call It Sleep (Roth), 37
Call of Stories, The (Coles), 29
Calloway, Cab, 131
Cambridge, Massachusetts, 33
Cambridge University, 77
Campion, Nardi Reeder, 5
Camus, Albert, 14, 29, 31, 36, 38–39,
   149
Cancer, 51–52
Capital punishment, 139, 140, 143
Cardozo, Benjamin N., 49, 119, 120,
   127
Carlyle, Thomas, 16
Carnegie Corporation of New York,
   162
Carr, Robert K., 133
Carson, Rachel, 44
Carter, Robert L., 133, 136

Carver, George Washington, 78
Carver, Raymond, 24
Catcher in the Rye, The (Salinger), 35, 46
Catholicism, 125, 146
Catullus, 26
Caulfield, Holden, 35, 46
Chambers v. Florida, 151
Character, 1, 3, 4, 11, 20, 45, 58, 64, 88, 111, 114, 120, 129–43, 150, 153, 162, 163, 164, 165, 170, 171, 172
Cheevy, Miniver, 56
Chekhov, Anton, 14, 44
Chemotherapy, 51
Chesnut, Mary, 170
Chicago Tribune, 164
Childhood and Society (Erikson), 13
Children of Crisis (Coles), 45
Children of Light and the Children of Darkness, The (Niebuhr), 14, 29
Children of the Ghetto (Zangwill), 9
Chopin, Kate, 170
Churchill, Sir Winston, 111, 116, 117, 165
Chutzpah (Dershowitz), 15
Cincinnatus, 113
Citizenship, 62, 80, 88, 94, 105, 107, 120, 124, 125, 128, 138
City and the Pillar, The (Vidal), 40
City of Mobile v. Bolton, 139
Civilization, 1, 46, 72, 82, 86, 88, 165
Civil rights, 12, 82, 96, 106, 133, 134, 164
Civil Rights Act, 96
Civil War, 45, 61, 66, 83, 141, 170

Clapham Committee, 73
Clark, Hunter R., 132
Clark, Kenneth B., 133
Clark, Tom C., 130
Cleveland, Grover, 4
Closing of the American Mind, The (Bloom), 56
Cold war, 1, 111, 149, 157, 163, 164
Coleman, William T., Jr., 133, 143
Coles, Robert, 28, 29, 37, 45

College: commencement, 3, 4, 28, 93, 94; convocation, 4, 28; degree, 22, 27, 28; degree requirements, 27; Ivy League, 13, 21, 25; land-grant, 84, 85; private, 30. *See also* Education, higher; University
Columbia Law School, 89
Common Law, The (Holmes), 45, 49
Common Law Tradition, The (Llewellyn), 15
Common Sense (Paine), 44
"Commonwealth of Liberal Learning, A" (Freedman), 26
Communism, 111, 112, 124, 149, 157, 164, 169
Community and Polity: The Organizational Dynamics of American Jewry (Elazar), 127
Conformity, 2, 105–8, 150, 153, 157
Connell, Evan S., Jr., 32
Connoisseur, The (Connell), 32–33
Conrad, Joseph, 14, 36, 44, 45, 155
Conroy, Frank, 38
Conscience, 23, 86, 168
Conservativism, 55, 121, 122, 138
Constitution, 18, 49, 61, 85, 94, 124, 125, 130, 134, 135, 137, 139, 140, 141, 142, 143, 151, 152, 162; Eighth Amendment, 124, 140; Equal Protection Clause, 66; Fifteenth Amendment, 137; Fourteenth Amendment, 121, 126, 135, 142. *See also* Law, constitutional
Constitutional Convention, 51, 141
Contemplation, 28, 106, 107, 108, 150, 153, 167
Convocation. *See* College, convocation
Courts, 19, 58, 123, 130, 136, 137, 138, 140, 151
Cozzens, James Gould, 14, 17
Creativity, 46, 63, 69, 77, 79, 80, 87, 100, 105, 108, 117, 148, 150, 167, 170, 171
Crime and Punishment (Dostoyevsky), 36

Crisis and Legitimacy: The Administrative Process and American Government (Freedman), 18
Cromwell, Oliver, 55
Crozer Theological Seminary, 152
cummings, e. e., 14
Curley, James Michael, 39
Curriculum, 20, 23, 71, 74, 82, 84, 85, 86, 145, 150

Dana, Richard Henry, Jr., 85
Dance, 23
Dante Alighieri, 16
Dartmouth College, 1, 21, 25–29, 153, 157
Darwin, Charles, 80
David Copperfield (Dickens), 10, 35
da Vinci, Leonardo, 87
Davis, Michael D., 132
Dead Sea Scrolls, 171
Dean, James, 149
Death Be Not Proud (Gunther), 11
Death in the Family, A (Agee), 17, 39
"Death of a Traveling Salesman" (Welty), 150
Debate, 17, 63, 105
Declaration of Independence, 18, 61, 117, 119, 130, 141
Deledda, Grazia, 44
Delta Wedding (Welty), 150
Democracy in America (de Tocqueville), 81, 119, 126, 127
Depression, 132
Dershowitz, Alan M., 15
Destiny, 1, 3, 22, 30, 114, 116, 117, 126, 130, 131, 143, 150, 153
de Tocqueville, Alexis, 81, 119, 126, 127
Dewey, Thomas E., 164–65
Dial M for Murder (Knott), 12
Diary, 80, 84, 123, 124, 170
Dickens, Charles, 4, 14, 36, 45, 145
Diderot (Wilson), 45
Discipline, academic, 2, 70, 71, 73, 77, 86, 87, 88, 90, 99, 102, 108

Discrimination, 130, 131, 135, 136, 139, 140, 161, 164
Disraeli, Benjamin, 62
Diversity, 51, 63, 64, 65, 67, 73, 90, 142
DNA, 80
Doctor Faustus (Mann), 105
Donne, John, 36
Dorris, Michael, 29
Dostoyevsky, Fyodor, 14, 45
Double Helix, The (Watson), 80
Douglas, William O., 126, 138
Dove, Rita, 24, 28
Drama. *See* Playwright; Theater
Dreamers of the Ghetto (Zangwill), 9
Dred Scott decision, 130
Du Bois, W. E. B., 130, 161
Due process of law, 18, 121, 126, 135, 151
Dulles, John Foster, 157
Durkheim, Emile, 22

Eastern Europe, 27, 115, 116, 120
Edel, Leon, 45
Edelman, Marian Wright, 28
Edison, Thomas Alva, 78
Education: graduate, 19, 27, 28; higher, 4, 17, 21, 23, 25, 55, 56, 63, 64, 65, 70, 83, 84, 86, 87; liberal (*see* Arts); secondary, 11, 13, 15, 17, 22, 33, 36, 65, 82, 84, 85, 131, 163
Einstein, Albert, 12, 22
Eisenhower, Dwight D., 13, 149, 151
Elazar, Daniel J., 127
Eliot, T. S., 13–14, 31, 36, 149, 168, 170
Ellison, Ralph, 29
Ellmann, Richard, 45
Elmer Gantry (Lewis), 34
Emerson, Ralph Waldo, 9, 63, 84, 102, 168
Enemy of the People, An (Ibsen), 23
Engle, Paul, 146
Equality, 58, 61–67, 83, 96, 107, 116, 119, 127, 134, 137, 138, 139, 141, 142, 143
Erikson, Erik, 13

Essay on Johnson (Macaulay), 9
Essays, 29, 31, 39, 49, 85, 95, 102, 146, 156, 167–72
Ethan Frome (Wharton), 10
Ethics, 87
Eucken, Rudolf Christoph, 44
Euripides, 122
Evans, Maurice, 12
Everything That Rises Must Converge (O'Connor), 147
Exemplar, 3, 18, 43, 57, 70, 106, 108, 111, 114, 116, 117, 126, 129, 130, 146, 150, 151, 152, 153, 155
Existentialism, 13, 39, 57, 147, 149

Faber and Faber, 168
Faculty, 2, 12, 15, 17, 18, 19, 20, 24, 27, 28, 37, 57, 58, 63, 69, 70, 72, 127, 131, 136; recruitment of, 27, 123
Fairbank, John K., 28
Fair Deal, 164
Faith, 2, 3, 67, 86, 95, 120, 123, 141, 142, 147, 152
Fall, The (Camus), 39
Fascism, 161
Faulkner, William, 14, 17, 23, 31, 36, 45
Feiffer, Jules, 149
Feminine Mystique, The (Friedan), 44
Ferguson, Robert A., 85
Fiction, 31, 45, 52, 145, 146
Fielding, Henry, 129
Finn, Huckleberry, 44
Finnegans Wake (Joyce), 14, 170
Fitzgerald, F. Scott, 50, 169
Foreign Affairs, 156
Foreign policy, 156, 157, 158, 159, 164
Forster, E. M., 14, 31, 36
Fortas, Abe, 119
Four Quartets (Eliot), 36
France, 20, 38, 163, 169
France, Anatole, 10
Franco, Francisco, 169
Frankenthaler, Helen, 28
Frankfurter, Felix, 12, 16, 17, 58, 95, 119, 120, 121, 123–26, 127, 128

Franklin, Benjamin, 51, 78
Franklin, John Hope, 133
Frederick the Great, 35
Freud, Sigmund, 9, 12, 13
Freund, Paul A., 15, 126
Friedan, Betty, 44
Friedländer, Saul, 38
Friend in Power, A (Baker), 21
Frost, Robert, 4, 30, 44
Frye, Northrup, 13
Fuentes, Carlos, 28

Galapagos Islands, 80
Galbraith, John Kenneth, 1, 13
Gant, Eugene, 71
Garden Party, The (Havel), 112
Gardner, Richard N., 89
Gellhorn, Walter, 15, 133
George Kennan and the Dilemmas of U.S. Foreign Policy (Mayers), 5
"Geranium, The" (O'Connor), 146
Ghana, 131
Gibbon, Edward, 16, 44
GI Bill of Rights, 90
Gide, André, 14, 31, 36
Gilbert, Peter A., 5
Gissing, George, 10
Glück, Louise, 27
Goethe, Johann Wolfgang, 105, 122
Goldberg, Arthur J., 119
Golden Treasury, The (Palgrave), 10
Goldstein, Joseph, 13
"Good Country People" (O'Connor), 147
Good Man Is Hard to Find, A (O'Connor), 29, 39, 147
Gorbachev, Mikhail, 158, 159
Gradgrind, Thomas, 145, 148
Grant, Mary Lynn, 5
Grant, Ulysses S., 170
Grass, Günter, 31, 116
"Great books," 40, 56, 74, 146. *See also* Reading, list
Great Britain, 20, 73
Greenberg, Jack, 133
Greene, Graham, 31, 40

Gregg v. Georgia, 140
Gregorian, Vartan, 20, 28, 86
Griswold, Erwin N., 133
Guerard, Albert J., 14
Gunther, John, 11

Halberstam, David, 45
Hamilton, Alexander, 85
Hamlet, 3
Hand, Learned, 16, 17, 55, 58, 101, 138
Hanover, New Hampshire, 31, 33
Hard Times (Dickens), 145
Hardy, Thomas, 14, 22
Harlan, John Marshall, 17, 138
Harriman, Averell, 11
Harrington, Michael, 45
Hart, H. L. A., 15
Hartz, Louis, 14
Harvard College, 11, 12, 13, 14, 15, 21, 29, 36
Harvard Law School, 58, 120, 123, 126, 131
Harvard University, 161
Hastie, William H., 138
Havel, Václav, 3, 47, 111–14, 116, 117, 149
Hawkes, John, 14, 37
Hawthorne, Nathaniel, 9, 158
Heaney, Seamus, 28
Heat and Dust (Jhabvala), 39
Hedgehog and the Fox, The (Berlin), 13
Helsinki Covenant on Civil and Political Rights, 112
Hemingway, Ernest, 4, 14, 31, 35, 36, 113
Henkin, Louis, 126
Henry James (Edel), 45
Hepburn, Katharine, 12
Heroism, 3, 11, 16, 28, 106, 111, 130, 146, 148, 149, 150, 153, 155, 159, 161, 170
Hertzberg, Arthur, 120, 121, 124
Heyse, Paul Johann Ludwig von, 44
Higginbotham, A. Leon, Jr., 28

Higher education. *See* Education, higher
Higher Learning in America, The (Veblen), 18
High school. *See* Education, secondary
Hinrichs, Gustavus, 73
Hispanic, 61, 62
History of the Decline and Fall of the Roman Empire, The (Gibbon), 44
Hitler, Adolf, 34, 35, 38
Hofstadter, Richard, 13, 14, 117
Hollow Men, The (Eliot), 149
Holmes, Oliver Wendell, Jr., 18, 19, 25, 32, 33, 45, 49, 93, 94, 102, 170
Holocaust, 1
Homer, 16
House of the Seven Gables, The (Hawthorne), 10
Houston, Charles Hamilton, 131, 132, 141
Howard Law School, 131, 132
Howard University, 65, 161, 162
Howells, William Dean, 10
Hudson, W. H., 10
Hue and Cry (McPherson), 39
Hufstedler, Shirley, 88
Hughes, Charles Evans, 125
Hughes, Langston, 131
Human Condition, The (Arendt), 22
Humanities, 73, 78, 80, 82, 85
Human rights, 112
Hume, David, 16, 22

Ibsen, Henrik, 14, 23
Idealism, 3, 18, 28, 29, 63, 67, 105, 111–14, 116, 120, 125, 127, 128, 129, 130, 135, 149
Identity, 2, 11, 12, 23, 28, 38, 100, 102, 113, 119, 120, 123, 130, 131, 147, 153
Idylls of the King (Tennyson), 10
Imagination, 2, 23, 29, 33, 34, 43, 44, 45, 79, 80, 87, 112, 114, 145–48, 151, 170
Imported Bridegroom and Other Stories of the New York Ghetto, The (Cahan), 10

Increased Difficulty of Concentration, The (Havel), 112
Individualism, 2, 13, 106
Industrial Revolution, 77, 145
Inman, Bobby Ray, 89
Institution, educational, 2, 11, 23, 27, 55, 64, 70, 83, 84, 85, 101, 152
Integration, racial, 137, 139, 143
Integrity, 57, 58, 159, 163, 169, 171, 172
Intellect, 23, 79, 112, 133, 171
Intellectual, 12, 74, 77, 106, 112, 114, 115–17, 120, 123, 133
Intellectualism, 15, 18, 20, 21, 22, 26, 27, 28, 30, 36, 39, 40, 46, 50, 56, 57, 58, 63, 65, 71, 72, 73, 74, 75, 77, 79, 80, 84, 87, 88, 95, 101, 117, 126, 127, 129, 138, 145, 146, 150, 151, 152, 153, 155, 156, 157, 158, 159, 161, 169, 170, 171, 172
International Ladies Garment Workers Union, 13
Interpretation of Dreams, The (Freud), 13
Invisible Man (Ellison), 29
Iowa City, 21, 31, 33
Iranian revolution, 89
Irving, John, 24, 37
Irving, Washington, 85
Israel, 20, 38, 113, 127, 164
It's Different at Dartmouth (Kemeny), 21
Ives v. South Buffalo Railroad Company, 18
Ivy League. *See* College

Jackson, Andrew, 4, 14
Jackson, Robert H., 125, 126
Jacob K. Javits Fellowship Program, 20
Jaffe, Louis L., 15
James, Henry, 4, 45
James, William, 145
James Joyce (Ellman), 45
Jefferson, Thomas, 32, 44, 55, 72, 85, 116, 117, 122, 123

Jehovah's Witness, 125
Jensen, Johannes Vilhelm, 44
Jewish Daily Forward, 10
Jews in America, The (Hertzberg), 120
Jhabvala, Ruth Prawer, 39
John Adams and the American Revolution (Bowen), 36
John Keats (Bate), 29, 45
Johnson, Edgar, 36
Johnson, Lyndon B., 65, 135, 151, 171
Johnson, Samuel, 9, 14, 32, 44, 134
Joseph Andrews (Fielding), 129
Journalism, 15, 21, 113, 146, 158, 164, 169
Joyce, James, 14, 44, 45, 170
Judaism, 9–10, 11, 12, 13, 29, 34–35, 38, 119, 120, 121, 123, 124, 125, 126, 127, 137
Judiciary, 18, 32, 81, 93, 94, 97, 119, 120, 122, 125, 126, 129, 133, 137, 151
Justice, 17, 18, 58, 61, 62, 64, 85, 107, 108, 120, 122, 127, 130, 136, 142, 143, 152, 153

Kafka, Franz, 149
Kant, Immanuel, 16
Kazin, Alfred, 13
Keats, John, 14, 29, 45, 146
Kelleher, John V., 14
Kelly, Walt, 149
Kemeny, Jean A., 21
Kemeny, John G., 21
Kennan, George F., 3, 14, 111, 155–59
Kennedy, Anthony, 139
Kennedy, John F., 15, 135, 137, 151
Keynes, John Maynard, 13, 80
Kierkegaard, Sören, 152
King, Cyrus, 32
King, Martin Luther, Jr., 3, 116, 117, 150, 152–53
King Lear (Shakespeare), 23
Kluger, Richard, 61
Knowledge, 2, 18, 21, 43, 47, 56, 63, 69–75, 79, 83, 84, 86, 87, 95, 99, 100, 101, 102, 122, 135, 161, 162

Korean War, 149, 164
Ku Klux Klan, 151

Landis, James M., 95
Language, 43, 45, 49, 50, 63, 82, 88, 89,
    113, 114, 115, 116, 117, 132, 147,
    168, 171; Arabic, 72; English, 4, 10,
    16, 89; foreign, 24, 32, 88, 89, 112;
    German, 121, 122, 123; Hebrew,
    126; Russian, 156; Yiddish, 10
Lasswell, Harold, 81
Last Hurrah, The (O'Connor), 39,
    40
Late George Apley, The (Marquand),
    78
Lathem, Edward Connery, 5
Law, 15, 16, 17, 18, 19, 21, 25, 33, 58,
    78, 80, 81–91, 93–97, 106, 107, 119,
    121, 126, 127, 129, 130, 135, 139,
    140, 142, 151, 164; administrative,
    18; constitutional, 16, 120, 121, 152;
    criminal, 135; family, 18
Law and Letters in American Culture
    (Ferguson), 85
"Law and Literature" (Cardozo), 49
Law clerk, 17, 122, 126, 136, 137, 139,
    141, 152
"Law Like Love" (Auden), 93
Lawrence, D. H., 14, 36
Law review, 18, 136. See also *Yale Law
    Journal*
Law school, 15, 16, 17, 18, 20, 21, 81,
    85, 86, 93, 127, 131, 136
Lawyer, 15, 16, 18, 20, 22, 25, 27, 45,
    49, 81, 82, 83, 85, 86, 87, 89, 90, 91,
    93, 94, 95, 96, 97, 106, 119, 126, 129,
    130, 131, 132, 133, 134, 136, 151
Leadership, 3, 15, 20, 35, 49, 62, 63,
    77, 78, 79, 81, 83, 87, 90, 91, 99, 108,
    111, 112, 113, 114, 115, 117, 119,
    120, 121, 123, 126, 127, 128, 143,
    150, 153, 158, 163
Leaf Storm (Marquez), 40
Learning, 2, 9, 11, 12, 14, 16, 18, 19,
    21, 22, 29, 46, 47, 51, 56, 67, 75,
    77–80, 81, 85

Least Dangerous Branch, The (Bickel),
    16, 58
Leavis, F. R., 56
Lee, Harper, 17
Lee, Robert E., 170
"Legal Education and Public Policy:
    Professional Training in the Public
    Interest" (Lasswell and McDougal),
    81
Lenin, Vladimir Ilyich, 170
Letter from Birmingham Jail (King),
    152
Lewis, Sinclair, 17, 34
Liberalism, 55, 57, 130
Library, 31, 32, 34, 36, 43, 44, 46, 47,
    69, 71, 100
*Life and Letters of Jean-Jacques
    Rousseau, The,* 10
Lincoln, Abraham, 4, 32, 45, 61, 108,
    114, 116–17, 124, 134, 143, 170
Lippmann, Walter, 164
Literary criticism, 14, 87, 168, 169,
    170, 171
Literature, 2, 9, 10, 36, 40, 43, 46, 63,
    85, 86, 87, 88, 114, 168, 170, 171
Lives (Plutarch), 129, 170
Llewellyn, Karl N., 15
Locke, John, 22, 116
London, 9, 34
Lonely Crowd, The (Riesman), 45, 149
Lord Jim (Conrad), 155
Louisville, Kentucky, 120
Lowell, Robert, 31, 171
Lowry, Malcolm, 36
Luther, Martin, 46, 108

Macaulay, Thomas Babington, 9, 152,
    163
Macbeth (Shakespeare), 10
Machiavelli, Niccolò, 16
Macklin, Charles, 93
MacLeish, Archibald, 36, 46, 113,
    119
Madison, James, 85, 97
Main Street (Lewis), 34
Maitland, Frederic William, 16

Making of the President, The (White), 45

Malamud, Bernard, 150

Male Animal, The (Thurber and Nugent), 12

Malinski v. New York, 58

Malraux, André, 14

Manchester, New Hampshire, 11, 12, 33, 34

Manhattan Project, 164

Mann, Thomas, 31, 36, 105, 109, 116

Mansfield, Lord, 85

Mansion, The (Faulkner), 17

Mantle of Elijah, The (Zangwill), 9

Marquand, John P., 78

Marquez, Gabriel Garcia, 40

Marshall, John, 32, 49

Marshall, Thurgood, 3, 17, 106–7, 108, 129–43, 164

Marshall Plan, 82, 156, 164

Martinson, Harry, 44

Marx, Karl, 13, 170

Massey, Paul, 23

Masters, The (Snow), 21

Mathematics, 24, 72, 102

Matthiessen, F. O., 13

Maturity, 2, 15, 25, 38, 114, 137, 152, 158

Maugham, W. Somerset, 34

Mayers, David, 5

Mayflower, The, 13

McCarthyism, 111, 164

McClintock, Barbara, 78

McCulloch v. Maryland, 49

McCullough, David, 163

McDougal, Myers, 81

McGrory, Mary, 165

McLaurin v. Oklahoma State Regents, 137

McPherson, James Alan, 24, 39

Melting Pot, The (Zangwill), 9

Melville, Herman, 23

Memoirs (Kennan), 157, 158

Memorandum, The (Havel), 112

Mencken, H. L., 171

Mentor, 27, 29, 70

Merk, Frederick, 14

Metaphysics, 29, 36, 38

Meyerson, Martin, 20

Meyer v. Nebraska, 121, 122

Milledgeville, Georgia, 29, 148

Miller, Arthur, 14

Miller, Perry, 14

Milliken v. Bradley, 139

Millionairess, The (Shaw), 12

Milosz, Czeslaw, 37

Milton, John, 14, 16, 22, 36–37, 45, 85

Minersville School District v. Gobitis, 125

Miss Lonelyhearts (West), 38, 40

Missouri ex rel. Gaines v. Canada, 137

Modern Library, 10, 34, 35, 36

Montaigne, Michel, 16, 168

Moon and Sixpence, The (Maugham), 34

Moon Is Blue, The (Herbert), 12

Moot court competition, 15, 17

Moral Essays (Pope), 9

Morality, 2, 17, 29, 39, 40, 49, 56, 57, 58, 64, 78, 79, 80, 83, 107, 108, 112, 113, 114, 116, 117, 120, 121, 122, 123, 126, 128, 129, 134, 140, 143, 145, 146, 150, 152, 153, 155, 157, 163, 165, 169

Morehouse College, 152

Morgan v. Virginia, 137

Morrill Act, 84

Mortality, 33, 51

Motivation, 3, 11, 65, 66

Motley, Constance Baker, 133

Mr. Valiant-for-Truth, 126

"Mr. X article" (Kennan), 156

Murray, Gilbert, 122

Music, 16, 22, 23, 24, 63, 65, 86, 105, 106

Myrdal, Gunnar, 45, 133, 134, 162

"Myth of Sisyphus, The" (Camus), 39

NAACP, 129, 131, 132, 135, 137

Nabokov, Vladimir, 44

National Labor Relations Board, 96

Nation at Risk, A (National Commission on Excellence in Education), 82

Natural, The (Malamud), 150
Natural selection, 80
Nazism, 35, 123, 125
Nevins, Allan, 83
New Deal, 82, 95, 126, 164
New Haven, Connecticut, 17, 33
Newman, John Henry, 72, 87
New Republic, 169
New State Ice Company v. Liebmann,
    49
Newton, Isaac, 72, 80
New Yorker, 169–70
New York Times, 89
Niebuhr, Reinhold, 14, 29, 149, 152
Nietzsche, Friedrich Wilhelm, 170
Nineteen Eighty-Four (Orwell), 115,
    168
Nixon, Richard M., 137, 138, 151
Nkrumah, Kwame, 131
Nobel Prize, 13, 161, 162
Nonviolence, 152
Norman, Jessye, 28
North Atlantic Treaty Organization,
    156–57, 164
Northwest Ordinance, 83
Novel, 13, 14, 17, 21, 29, 32, 34, 36, 38,
    39, 51, 62, 79, 85, 129, 145, 146, 147,
    149, 150, 168, 171
Nugent, Elliott, 12

Obligation, 2, 3, 44, 63, 64, 79, 82, 86,
    101, 105, 107, 113, 117, 121, 125,
    131, 136, 163
O'Casey, Sean, 14
O'Connor, Edwin, 39
O'Connor, Flannery, 3, 24, 29, 39,
    146–48
O'Connor, Sandra Day, 140–41
Of Human Bondage (Maugham), 34
Of Time and the River (Wolfe), 71
Olmsted, Frederick Law, 170
Ombudsman, 19–20
Omeros (Walcott), 12
O'Neill, Eugene, 10, 14
One-person, one-vote, 16
One Writer's Beginnings (Welty), 151

Optimist's Daughter, The (Welty),
    150
Organization Man, The (Whyte), 149
Ortega y Gasset, José, 87
Orthodoxy, 11, 69, 73, 112, 169
Orwell, George, 3, 115, 168–69, 171
Other America, The (Harrington), 45

Paine, Thomas, 44
Painting, 23, 79
Paley, Grace, 27
Parkman, Francis, 85
Parks, Rosa, 153
Pasternak, Boris, 47, 116
Patriotic Gore (Wilson), 170, 171
Peace Corps, 82
Pei, I. M., 28
Pelikan, Jaroslav, 101
People and the Court, The (Black),
    15
Phi Beta Kappa, 15
Philadelphia, 20, 21, 31, 33, 141, 142
Philosophy, 26, 86, 87, 106, 112, 120,
    122, 125, 126, 146, 147, 149, 152,
    153, 167; educational, 74, 145; legal,
    58
Pilgrim's Progress, The (Bunyan),
    126
Plague, The (Camus), 29, 38–39, 40
Plato, 16, 22, 112
Playwright, 36, 93, 111, 112, 116, 149,
    171
Plutarch, 129, 163, 170
Poe, Edgar Allan, 9
Poetry, 14, 16, 25, 26, 27, 29, 30, 31,
    36, 37, 40, 43, 46, 63, 72, 78, 79, 80,
    85, 100, 106, 116, 119, 122, 123, 150,
    155, 170, 171
Poland, 20, 115
Political correctness, 70, 172
Politics, 2, 39, 96, 107, 112, 113, 114,
    115, 117, 123, 135, 140, 152, 153,
    158, 163, 165, 168, 169, 171
"Politics and the English Language"
    (Orwell), 169
Pollak, Louis H., 13, 15, 133

Pontoppidan, Henrik, 44
Pope, Alexander, 9
Potsdam conference, 165
Prejudice, 66, 121, 142, 151
Pride and Prejudice (Austen), 73
Prime of Miss Jean Brodie, The
  (Spark), 17
Prince Philip, Duke of Edinburgh, 131
Princeton University, 131, 155, 156,
  157, 169
*Principles, Politics, and Fundamental
  Law* (Wechsler), 16
Pritchett, V. S., 168
"Private Lives and Public Institu-
  tions," 22
Private View, A (Havel), 112
"Prospective Overruling and Retroac-
  tive Application in the Federal
  Courts" (Freedman), 17
Prospero, 26, 47
*Protestant Ethic and the Spirit of Capi-
  talism, The* (Weber), 23
Proust, Marcel, 44, 170
Pulitzer Prize, 157

Queen Elizabeth, 35

Rabelais, François, 16
Racism, 12, 65, 142
Ralph Bunche—An American Life
  (Urquhart), 162
Rauschenbusch, Walter, 14
Ravitch, Diane, 90
Rawls, John, 58
Reading, 9, 10, 12, 14, 16, 17, 21, 24,
  29, 32, 34, 35, 36, 37, 38, 39, 40, 43,
  45, 46, 57, 63, 99, 100, 108; list, 22,
  39, 56, 69, 146, 147, 163, 165, 167.
  See also "Great books"
Real Thing, The (Stoppard), 40
Rebel, The (Camus), 39
Rebel Without A Cause, 149
Red and the Black, The (Stendahl), 36
Reflection, 29, 56, 70, 105, 106, 108,
  113, 129, 142, 152, 164, 165
"Reflections on Gandhi" (Orwell), 169

Reflections on the Revolution in France
  (Burke), 22
*Regents of the University of California
  v. Bakke,* 66, 140
Rehnquist, William H., 138
Religion, 2, 11, 21, 63, 78, 83, 87, 120,
  123, 124, 125, 147, 152, 167. *See also*
  Catholicism; Jehovah's Witness;
  Judaism
Research, 69, 78, 100, 102
Return of the Native, The (Hardy),
  46
"Reverse discrimination," 140
Revolt of the Masses, The (Ortega y
  Gasset), 87
Rhodes Scholarship, 28
Riesman, David, 45
Rise of David Levinsky, The (Cahan),
  10
Robber Bridegroom, The (Welty), 150
Robinson, Edwin Arlington, 56
Robinson, Spottswood W., III, 133
Roosevelt, Eleanor, 108
Roosevelt, Franklin D., 11, 14, 32,
  123, 124, 126, 151, 163, 165
Roosevelt, Theodore, 32
Rostov, Natasha, 35
Rostow, Eugene V., 15
Roth, Henry, 37
Roth, Philip, 27
Rushdie, Salman, 47
Russia, 156, 170
Russian Revolution, 168, 170

Salinger, J. D., 35, 46, 149
Salk, Jonas, 12, 28, 78
Sanchez, Oscar Arias, 28
Sandburg, Carl, 99, 108, 114
Sartre, Jean-Paul, 14, 36, 149
Scalia, Antonin, 139
Schlesinger, Arthur M., Jr., 14
Schneiderman v. United States, 124
Scholar, 9, 11, 14, 15, 16, 18, 20, 21,
  27, 28, 46, 49, 58, 72, 74, 75, 87, 100,
  101, 102, 106, 108, 126, 133, 136,
  145, 157

Scholarship, 11, 18, 27, 100, 101, 102, 133, 157, 162
Schorer, Mark, 17
Schreiner, Olive, 10
Schumpeter, Joseph, 14
Sciences, 1, 2, 24, 27, 63, 72, 77–80, 84, 86, 87, 88, 93, 100, 102, 112, 146, 147, 168
Scott, Sir Walter, 45
Segregation, 16, 45, 61, 131, 134, 137, 142, 152, 161, 162, 164
Self, 1, 2, 3, 12, 28, 51, 105–9, 120, 124, 130, 151, 152, 153, 167
Sermons Preached in a University Church (Buttrick), 14
Service, 3, 18, 20, 37, 89, 93, 94, 95, 96, 97, 105, 107, 113, 117, 124, 126, 127, 129, 134, 135, 136, 145, 151, 162
Sexism, 12
Shakespeare, William, 4, 9, 16, 22, 26, 37, 43, 47, 85, 146
Shaw, George Bernard, 4, 12, 14, 36
Shelley, Percy Bysshe, 116
Shelley v. Kraemer, 137
Sherman, William T., 170
"Shooting an Elephant" (Orwell), 169
Silas Marner (Eliot), 10
Silent Spring (Carson), 44
Simple Justice (Kluger), 61
Sincerity and Authenticity (Trilling), 150
Singer, Isaac Bashevis, 74
Skeffington, Frank, 39
Smiley, Jane, 24
Smith v. Allwright, 137
Snow, C. P., 21, 77, 80
Socialism, 169, 170
Social Science Research Council, 73
Social sciences, 20, 78, 80, 86
Social Thought in America (White), 14
Socrates, 15, 168
Solow, Robert M., 28
Solzhenitsyn, Aleksandr, 28, 47, 116
Souls of Black Folk, The (Du Bois), 130

Sovereign Prerogative, The (Rostow), 15
Soviet Union, 88, 90, 111, 115, 149, 155, 156, 158, 163, 164
Spark, Muriel, 17
Specialization, 2, 24, 33, 73, 83, 86, 87, 89, 95, 101, 135
Spender, Stephen, 155
Spitteler, Carl Friedrich George, 44
Sputnik, 90
Stafford, William, 24
Stalin, Joseph, 169
State Universities and Democracy, The (Nevins), 83
Status, social, 11, 58
Steele, Richard, 168
Stegner, Wallace, 24
Steiker, Carol, 135
Stein, Gertrude, 170
Steiner, George, 115
Stellar, Eliot, 20
Stevens, Wallace, 14
Stoppard, Tom, 40, 112
Stop-time (Conroy), 38, 40
Stowe, Harriet Beecher, 45, 170
Strand, Mark, 27
Stranger, The (Camus), 39
Sumner, William Graham, 14
Supreme Court, 45, 61, 62, 119, 122, 123, 124, 125, 126, 129, 134, 136, 137, 138, 139, 141, 142, 143, 152, 162; justice, 15, 17, 18, 107, 119, 121, 123, 129, 130, 135, 151, 171
Sweatt v. Painter, 137
Sybil (Disraeli), 62

Tacitus, 152
Talmud, 11
Taney, Roger B., 130
Taylor, Kressman, 34
Teaching, 9, 10, 11, 12, 14, 15, 16, 18, 20, 21, 22, 25, 29, 34, 35, 38, 49, 55–59, 69, 74, 75, 86, 96, 99, 100, 102, 106, 108, 125, 126, 131, 132, 145, 146, 147, 165
Tel Aviv University, 38

Tennyson, Alfred Lord, 17
Tenure, 19, 69, 99, 101, 119, 126, 135
Thacher, George J., 73
Theater, 13, 14, 22, 23, 51, 63, 86, 106, 112, 113
Thomas, Dylan, 14
Thoreau, Henry David, 31, 171
Thucydides, 16
Thurber, James, 168
Thurgood Marshall: Warrior at the Bar, Rebel on the Bench (Davis and Clark), 132
Tillich, Paul, 152
Time magazine, 134
To Kill a Mockingbird (Lee), 17
Tolstoy, Lev Nikolaevich, 44
To Reclaim a Legacy (Bennett), 82
To the Finland Station (Wilson), 170
Tradition, 2, 49, 63, 72, 78, 80, 81, 85, 86, 128, 150
Transcendentalists, 14
Trilling, Lionel, 150, 169
Trop v. Dulles, 124
Trotsky, Leon, 170
Troubled Crusade, The (Ravitch), 90
Truffaut, François, 149
Truman, Harry S., 3, 4, 111, 151–52, 161, 162–65
Truman (McCullough), 163
Truman Doctrine, 156, 164
Twain, Mark, 4, 40, 44, 45
"Two Cultures and the Scientific Revolution, The" (Snow), 77
Two Jewish Justices: Outcasts in the Promised Land (Burt), 120

Ulysses (Joyce), 14, 170
Uncle Tom's Cabin (Stowe), 45
Undergraduate, 12, 13, 14, 23, 24, 27, 36, 38, 39, 57, 85, 86, 87, 150, 162, 165
United Nations, 82, 161, 162, 164
United States v. Kras, 135
University, 1, 3, 17, 18, 19, 20, 21, 22, 23, 24, 25, 37, 43, 46, 49, 50, 62, 65, 67, 69, 70, 73, 74, 81, 82, 83, 84, 85, 87, 88, 89, 99, 102, 123, 140, 161; Big Ten, 13, 21; public, 21, 29, 64. *See also* College; Education, higher
University of California at Los Angeles, 161
University of Iowa, 1, 20, 21, 22, 23–25, 27, 37, 38, 73, 146; Law School, 20; Writers' Workshop, 24, 25, 37, 38, 146
University of Maryland Law School, 131, 132
University of Pennsylvania Law School, 17–18, 20, 21, 29
Unsilent Generation, The, 149
Urquhart, Brian, 162

Valéry, Paul, 170
Values, 3, 4, 15, 18, 20, 25, 28, 29, 55–59, 81, 84, 87, 88, 89, 91, 94, 96, 99, 107, 108, 115, 116, 125, 143, 163, 165
Vanity Fair, 169
Veblen, Thorstein, 18, 23
Vendler, Helen, 28
Vicar of Wakefield, The (Goldsmith), 40
Vidal, Gore, 40
Vietnam War, 45, 89, 157
Violent Bear It Away, The (O'Connor), 147
Vocation, 79, 85, 99, 101, 157
Voting, 137, 138, 139, 142
Voting Rights Act, 96

Wagner Act, 96
Walcott, Derek, 12, 27, 28
Walesa, Lech, 149
War and Peace (Tolstoy), 35
War on Poverty, 82
Warren, Earl, 62, 124, 134, 138
Warren, Robert Penn, 31
Warsaw Pact, 112–13
Washington, George, 4, 126
Washington Post, 89
Waste Land, The (Eliot), 36, 149
Watson, James, 80

Weber, Max, 22, 23
Wechsler, Herbert L., 16
Week on the Concord and Merrimack Rivers, A (Thoreau), 31
Wells, H. G., 10
Welty, Eudora, 3, 150–51, 153
West, Mae, 69
West, Nathanael, 38
Western civilization, 72, 88, 165
Western Europe, 164
West Virginia State Board of Education v. Barnette, 125
Wharton, Edith, 4, 10
What Makes Sammy Run? (Schulberg), 36
When Memory Comes (Friedländer), 38, 40
Where Has All the Ivy Gone? (Beadle), 21
White, E. B., 168
White, Morton, 14
White, Theodore H., 45
Whitehead, Alfred North, 22
"Why I Live at the P. O." (Welty), 150
Wilbur, Richard, 27
Wilder, Thornton, 35
Williams, Tennessee, 14, 24
Williams, William Carlos, 25
Wilson, Angus, 37
Wilson, Arthur, 45
Wilson, August, 28

Wilson, Edmund, 3, 31, 168, 169–72
Wilson, James, 18, 85
Wilson, Woodrow, 119, 121
Wise Blood (O'Connor), 146
Wolfe, Thomas, 71
Women's movement, 45
Woodward, C. Vann, 133
Woolf, Virginia, 4, 11, 36, 168
Workmen's compensation, 18
World War I, 121, 157, 163, 169
World War II, 29, 38, 73, 88, 115, 116, 156, 163
"Worn Path, A" (Welty), 150
Writers' Workshop. *See* University of Iowa
Writing, 10, 13, 15, 19, 23, 24, 25, 26, 27, 28, 35, 36, 37, 39, 40, 41, 43, 44, 45, 46, 79, 107, 112, 114, 115, 132, 146, 147, 148, 150, 167, 168, 170
Wythe, George, 85

Yale Law Journal, 17
Yale Law School, 11, 12, 15, 17, 21, 29, 85, 106. *See also* Law school
Yeats, William Butler, 14, 72, 107, 111, 170
Yellow Raft in Blue Water, A (Dorris), 29
Young, Edward, 150, 153

Zangwill, Israel, 9, 13
Zionism, 120, 121, 123